OUR SPIRITUAL WAKE-UP CALLS

OUR SPIRITUAL WAKE-UP CALLS

HAROLD KLEMP

MAHANTA TRANSCRIPTS
BOOK 15

ECKANKAR
Minneapolis

Printed in U.S.A.

Compiled by Mary Carroll Moore
Edited by Joan Klemp and Anthony Moore
Text illustrations by Catherine Purnell
Text photo (page xii) by Robert Huntley
Back cover photo by Robert Huntley

Second printing—1999

Library of Congress Cataloging-in-Publication Data

Klemp, Harold.
   Our spiritual wake-up calls / Harold Klemp.
      p. cm. — (Mahanta transcripts ; bk. 15)
   Includes index.
   ISBN 1-57043-135-3 (alk. paper)
   1. Eckankar (Organization)—Doctrines. 2. Spiritual life—Eckankar (Organization.) I. Title. II. Series: Klemp, Harold. Mahanta transcripts ; bk. 15.
BP605.E3K5646 1997
230'.993—dc21   97-30917
                                          CIP

♾ The paper used in this publication meets the minimum requirements of the American National Standard for Information Sciences — Permanence of Paper for Printed Library Materials, ANSI Z39.48-1984.

CONTENTS

More Conscious • "I Love You, I Love You" • We Keep
Growing • Learning about Life • A Better Return

FOREWORD

The teachings of ECK define the nature of Soul. You are Soul. You are like a star of God sent into this world for spiritual experience. That will purify you.

Karma and reincarnation are thus primary beliefs in ECK. Your goal in this lifetime should be spiritual freedom. After that, you become a Coworker with God, both here and in the next world.

Key to the ECK teachings is the Mahanta, the Living ECK Master. He indeed acts as both the Outer and Inner Master for ECK students. The prophet of Eckankar, he is given respect but is not worshiped. He teaches the sacred name of God, HU. When sung just a few minutes each day, HU will lift you spiritually into the Light and Sound of God—to the ECK (Holy Spirit). This easy spiritual exercise and others will purify you. You are then able to accept the full love of God in this very lifetime.

Sri Harold Klemp is the Mahanta, the Living ECK Master today. Author of many books, discourses, and articles, he teaches the ins and outs of the spiritual life. His teachings lift people and help them recognize and understand their own experiences in the Light and Sound of God. Many of his talks are available to you on audio- and videocassette.

Our Spiritual Wake-Up Calls, Mahanta Transcripts, Book 15, contains his talks from 1995 to 1996. May they help you recognize how you are in the grasp of divine love every moment of every day.

Sri Harold Klemp, the Mahanta, the Living ECK Master, speaking in Montreal, Quebec, Canada, reminds everyone that, "All of you are in the grasp of divine love. All the time, every day, no matter where you go."

1

DO YOU HAVE TROUBLE LOVING GOD?

I was reading in a newspaper several weeks ago that when a public speaker begins speaking, he should not waste time thanking the audience for being there. But I like to do that. Because what's the hurry?

We run from morning till night; we have so many very important things to do. And running like this from morning till night, fifty, sixty, seventy, eighty years, or more pass. And the more years, the quicker they seem to pass. Unless somewhere along the line, we have become grounded in something. Otherwise, at the end of that time you ask yourself, Was it worth it? Was this voyage worth the trouble?

The thing that fills in the blank space is divine love. So the title for this evening's talk is "Do You Have Trouble Loving God?"

SLOWING DOWN

The last two years have been a very interesting experience for me personally. I've been having all kinds of interesting bouts with my health — as many of you have at one time or another. But one of the changes that came is that I have not watched television or used a computer for two years.

At first I wondered,

At first I wondered, *What am I going to do with my time? No computer, no television. How am I going to get along?* Thankfully, there's still radio. Or for enjoyment in the evening, I'll read to my wife from a series of novels written by Patrick O'Brian. They are the Commodore series, novels about sea life in the British Royal Navy at the time of Napoleon. He has a very enjoyable insight into human nature, and the stories are good adventures.

At first I wondered, What am I going to do with my time? No computer, no television. How am I going to get along?

This is how I spent some of my voyage over the past two years, reading about this sea adventure and the friendship between a captain in the Royal Navy and the surgeon on his ship. This surgeon also happens to be a spy for the British Empire, and it makes a very nice mix. There are seventeen of the novels, so plenty of time, plenty to read.

The friendship between these two characters is such a noble thing. They have the highest respect for each other.

Sometimes the captain is on a mission for the Royal Navy where he has to go out to one part of the world or another. The surgeon is also a naturalist, and he often wants to stop off at one of the nice little islands and check out the beetles. He wants to see all the little beetles and bugs; he thinks this is just what the voyage is all about. But the captain says to him, "We must pull up anchor; there is not a moment to be lost." That phrase repeats so often in the book. The surgeon-naturalist is entirely sick of hearing "not a moment to be lost."

One time, they were going around a very long, narrow island. The naturalist and a friend of his wanted to go ashore and look for bugs and beetles and birds. He asked the captain, "Since you're going to be traveling so slowly into the wind, why don't you just drop us off? We could walk across the island and meet you on the other side."

But the captain knew better. He had seen his friend the naturalist on an island where there was barely one species of bug. The naturalist became totally entranced and was lost for half a day.

They were in an area of the South Pacific with a lot of bugs, and the captain thought he would never finish his mission for the Royal Navy if he let this naturalist loose on this particular island. So the captain said, "There is not a moment to be lost." This was the end of any scientific explorations on that island as far as the naturalist was concerned.

The only thing that really matters is if we can find God's love sometime in this life.

A public speaker isn't supposed to say, "It's a pleasure to be here with you," as if someone is always whispering at him or her, "There is not a moment to be lost." But in the end, what does it matter? The only thing that really matters is if we can find God's love sometime in this life.

That's a Good Answer

At the 1995 ECK Springtime Seminar, I told the story of a mother who was preparing dinner for her family one evening, and her little boy came up and said, "Where do words comes from?" She was trying to think of an answer. "Oh, let's see," she said. Then the boy said, "There were words before there were people and dinosaurs." The mother said, "Well, maybe words came from dreams and HU." HU is an old name for God. "That's a good answer, Mommy," the boy told her.

In July, I got a letter from a mother in North

Carolina. She hadn't been to the seminar but was listening to the audiocassette of my talk, and she heard the story. "Hey, that's my story," she said. "But I didn't write about it to Harold, so how did he know?"

So she asked her husband, "Did you write to Harold about our son asking me where words came from?" He said he hadn't.

The woman felt very confused. She remembered she had been making supper one evening, when her son came in and said, "Mommy, where do words come from?" As she was trying to figure out what to say, the boy said, "There were words before there were dinosaurs."

"But there weren't any people before there were dinosaurs," the mother answered.

"But there were words before there were people and dinosaurs," her son told her. He was so definite. And she was very puzzled by this train of thought.

Then the boy asked again, "Well, where do they come from?" "Maybe you can find out from the Inner Master in a dream," she told him. "That's a good answer, Mom," he said.

The two stories were very close. Then it occurred to the woman that maybe on the inner planes there's a children's Satsang class, a spiritual study class. And at this class the Inner Master would tell the children, "OK, now sometime soon when your mother's making dinner at night, ask her where words come from. And after she tells you, then say, 'That's a very good answer, Mommy.'"

We occasionally see things like this happening, two instances where people have similar experiences. There are examples in history too.

CATCH THE WAVE HOME

We occasionally see things like this happening, two instances where people have similar experiences. There are examples in history too. People have invented the same products at the same time.

When you see this, you realize that there is a thread behind life. Something is going on. And it's more than meets the eye. You wonder, *What is this stream of continuity? What is the unifying element that binds all life together?* It is Divine Spirit. We call It the ECK.

Divine Spirit is the Voice of God, It is love coming from God. When we say God's Voice, we're talking about the expression of God's love flowing out to all creation.

The other aspect of this divine love is that it flows back home to God. The duty of Soul, at some point in Its evolution, is to catch this wave of love that's going home to God. To catch the wave, and ride it home.

The duty of Soul, at some point in Its evolution, is to catch this wave of love that's going home to God.

There have been a number of hurricanes this year. People in the weather-forecasting business recognize that this is an active year for hurricanes. At the time Hurricane Marilyn went through the Virgin Islands and devastated 80 percent of St. Thomas, an ECKist mother was returning from vacation with her husband. They heard about Hurricane Marilyn going across St. Thomas. Her son was living there at the time. And she was very, very worried about his safety.

In Eckankar people sometimes ask the Inner Master for assurance. So she said to the Mahanta, the Inner Master, "Is my son all right?" And the assurance came back to her, "He's all right, don't worry."

But being a mother, she was still very concerned.

That evening she and her husband were going to watch a college football game on television. At about 6:20, while she was making dinner, she suddenly got this impression from the Inner Master to turn on the television set. The game was going to start at 6:30. But as soon as she turned on the television, the announcer said, "After this break we'll bring the latest news coverage of the hurricane on St. Thomas." She called her husband, "Come quick, they're going to have some news about the hurricane."

So the husband and wife sat down in front of the television. And when the commercial was over, the television camera panned across the destruction on the island. It closed in on two people who were inspecting the damage during the hurricane. One of them was their son.

At this moment, the woman knew this was God's answer to her motherly concern so that she wouldn't worry anymore. She could see that her son was OK.

For the rest of evening, as more and more news reports came in, they never showed that particular clip again—the one with her son. Because after that it wasn't necessary.

Do you have trouble loving God?

WHEN WE HAVE TROUBLE TRUSTING GOD

Do you have trouble loving God? When times are good, the answer is no. But when we're under stress or when times are a little bit on the hard side, more often the answer is yes.

It's sometimes very difficult to trust in God when things are going against us.

Job in the Old Testament is a very good example. One catastrophe after another came to him. He lost everything that meant anything to him, his possessions and his family. His friends were trying to convince him that he should give up his love for this God that he believed in. But Job, through it all, kept his face toward God. And at the end his family and possessions were restored to him many times over. In other words, life may take from you, but it will always return the bounty in richer measure—if you have learned the spiritual lessons that were involved with your loss.

KARMA AND EARTH'S PEOPLES

Divine love flows through the Holy Spirit down to earth, even though you might wonder sometimes. There is so much war going on, in all different parts of the world. In the Mideast and on the dividing line between Europe and Asia, people have been at war for thousands of years. And whenever somebody gets the upper hand, they will go against some minority.

Back and forth, back and forth, they've been happily at it for these thousands of years. Making war on each other, killing each other, and harboring a grudge against the other side who retaliated. Because, of course, each side forgets its own atrocities.

We are so good at that ourselves. If someone slights us, we may not forget. But it never occurs to us that we may have caused a slight to the other person in the beginning.

What we're speaking of is karma, the cause and effect that takes place every day in the life of each individual on earth. It also takes place in the history of all peoples and all nations. There is individual karma, karma made by a person, but there is also karma made by communities and nations. It's a case of one party throwing a stone at the other party and the other party throwing a spear back. Then the first party launches some kind of catapult that throws a big rock. As the ages go by, man has found more effective and awesome ways to throw bigger rocks at his enemy.

Life may take from you, but it will always return the bounty in richer measure—if you have learned the spiritual lessons that were involved with your loss.

We see this warfare going on and want to ask these people, "Do you have trouble loving God?" There's a lot of religion behind this warfare—whether orthodox Christianity or Islam, the religion of the Muslims. Every path has its belligerent people, and every path has its peaceful people.

You want to ask the people who are so ready to make war, "Do you have trouble loving God?" Yet most of them would become very angry: How dare you raise the question?

So if you're wise, you won't ask. You know what the consequences will be. There's a lot of history here: what they have done to each other in the past. You can see that they're not going to change their habits, no matter how many dollars somebody stuffs in their pockets to have them quit fighting.

Divine Spirit also helps people in their personal lives. This is the area we are most concerned with.

But Divine Spirit also helps people in their personal lives. This is the area we are most concerned with. Not with the karma of nations, but with helping people understand how the karma they have made in the past has come back to them in this lifetime— and more importantly, what they can do about it.

SWEET TROUBLE

A member of ECK had had a very hard time with sweets her whole life. She just loved them. With her coffee she'd always want to have doughnuts. She loved pastry and cookies.

After a while she noticed that the sweets were having a very bad effect upon her. Eating sweets made her nervous and fearful. As soon as she went on one of her sugar binges, she'd feel very afraid. She'd get back to her apartment and slide a chair in front of the door because she was suddenly so afraid. In some people, too much sugar will have these effects.

It can make you frightened or angry.

About a year after she became a member of Eckankar, this woman learned at one of the Eckankar meetings that it's all right to ask Divine Spirit for help. You can ask the Mahanta, the Inner Master, "I would like help in breaking this habit of eating sweets in such huge quantities." She knew it was causing her problems in her spiritual life, and she wanted help. But she'd always had a feeling of being too lazy to do anything about her problem with eating sweets.

You can ask the Mahanta, the Inner Master, "I would like help in breaking this habit of eating sweets in such huge quantities."

That weekend, she was going to Yosemite National Park to meet some friends. Before she left, she filled up with cookies; when she got to the park, she went to the camp store and bought more crackers and cookies and other sweet things. She took all this back to the camping area.

That evening the group was sitting in their campsite, and the young daughter of one of the women was telling a story about something she had done in kindergarten. "Our teacher will read a story to us," the girl said, "and then she'll ask us questions to see if we understand what the story is about." Each time the teacher asks a student a question and the student is able to answer, the teacher gives the student a little goldfish cracker. She calls it brain food. It is a very good incentive for the students, because if they answer right, they get a little treat. The woman listened to the story, thinking, "Hmmm, that's a pretty good idea, a good way for a teacher to be teaching. When the student gets the answer right, give them a little treat."

That night as this woman was falling asleep in her sleeping bag, it dawned on her that she hadn't locked the food bin where she kept the sweets.

Yosemite has bears. But she was too lazy to get up and check.

Early in the morning, one of her friends heard a noise. "Either someone's having a midnight snack or that's a bear in our food," she said.

The woman was very scared. The friend got up and ran over to the food bin. A bear was sitting there, and it was eating all the cookies and candy, just enjoying itself very thoroughly. The friend took pots and pans, made a terrible racket, and finally drove the bear away. After the bear left, the woman was shaking. The little girl who had told her story earlier in the evening thought it was delightful—children sometimes don't understand the danger—because the bear had such a sad look on its face as it was leaving the candy and all the treats. It was as if the bear was saying, "Oh, please, can't you let me come back and finish? After all, I've touched it."

After they locked the food bin, the woman reached into her jacket pocket and pulled out this little gold-fish cracker. She had no idea how it got there.

But suddenly she made the connection: the experience was to teach her something about her attachment to sweets, that she had this "bear of an appetite" for sweets. And because she had realized what it meant, when she reached in her pocket, she got a treat from the Inner Master. The little cracker, the little goldfish that said, "You've done very well with your spiritual lesson this morning, so here's a little treat for you, here's a little brain food." And after that she joined Overeaters Anonymous, and she has been off sugar for quite a while.

These reforms are very, very difficult. Unless you can get to the cause of what's behind the problem. Unless you go back and find out what caused the

These reforms are very, very difficult. Unless you can get to the cause of what's behind the problem.

karma. Why does this woman have this enormous appetite for sweets? Where did it come from? Once she can understand that, then this craving for sugar can go away on its own.

EVERYDAY MIRACLES

People who need help sometimes get it in the most astonishing ways. And usually the connection between people and the help they receive is a bond of divine love. The theme repeats.

We study dreams in Eckankar. We pay a lot of attention to dreams. And I've written a series of dream discourses for the members of Eckankar. The study of dreams shows the connection between the divine and the mundane. There's a hidden connection between the visible and the invisible, and there's this place where the two meet. The two meet in our state of consciousness.

Some people find miracles all the time. Because life is like a sea. You're walking in a sea of experiences every moment of your life. And some people walking around in this sea of life find miracles every day. Other people are not even aware that such miracles exist, and they become very upset if you speak about miracles. If it's big and splashy, if it deserves some kind of front-page notice in the *National Enquirer,* people say, "That doesn't count because it's made up." And if it's a very small miracle, they say, "You're not going to say that there's a connection, are you?"

But in Eckankar we know about the waking dream. This is when something happens in your daily life that is a demonstration of a spiritual principle that you need to learn. You need to learn this principle to overcome or undo some karmic pattern that you have made in the past.

You're walking in a sea of experiences every moment of your life.

TO A HIGHER STATE

Why would anyone even want to get rid of karma? The answer is simple: So that you can open yourself to more love from God. This is the only reason.

You can't force people to become loving. It doesn't help to stuff money into the pockets of individuals and say, "If I give this to you, you're going to be much better off." Because if that person has a deep spiritual problem, perhaps of poverty, it probably won't be very long before that person will be back in poverty.

Or if a person has a certain kind of health problem and one of the healers takes it away, but the person doesn't learn anything from the healing and continues the habits that caused the illness, then the illness or one just like it is going to come back.

I often like to say that healing on earth is temporary. Some people are apt to say, "Yes, but Jesus did some real miracles. He raised people from the dead, healed the sick." But my point in saying that healing is temporary is this: people who were healed have since died. Even the people who were raised from the dead are now gone. So what was the point of the healing? Was it just to get rid of the sickness? Obviously the answer must be no. There must have been more to these healings.

A spiritual master can invite people to a higher level, but he can't force them.

If the purpose wasn't to heal, then what was it? It was to raise the state of consciousness.

You cannot force anyone into a higher state of consciousness. And Jesus couldn't either. And more important, he wouldn't. Because it's against the spiritual law to do so.

A spiritual master can invite people to a higher level, but he can't force them. Oh, he could if he didn't know the spiritual law. But he won't. Because he knows the spiritual laws.

Two Amazing Phone Calls

An ECKist was studying dreams, and one night in the dream state the Inner Master gave her two phone numbers. The only clue she had from the Mahanta, or the Dream Master (another descriptive title for the Mahanta is the Dream Master), was that one was a home number and the other was an office number. This happened on July 22.

When she woke up, she remembered the dream. But she felt strange calling these two phone numbers. How do you tell someone, "I just had a dream, and God told me to call your number"?

This reminds me of a Gary Larson cartoon in *The Far Side*. Gary Larson has very good insight into human nature. In this one cartoon, the phone rings. A man picks it up. He's in his living room. A voice says, "Hello, this is God." The man in the living room asks who God wants to speak to. God mentions a name, and the man answers that he is sorry but God has reached the wrong number. The caption underneath reads: After that, he never stopped telling people that he had talked to God. But it was a wrong number of course.

So finally, about a month later the ECKist called the first number. She got an answering machine and left a message, "Please call me when you can. I got your number and I would like to make a connection here." Then she called the second number and left the same basic message on that answering machine.

The next day she got a call from a woman. The woman said, "I got your phone message. What is it exactly that you want to know?" So the ECKist explained. She said, "I had this dream, and in the dream I got your phone number. Is there any connection that you might make from this?" And so the

How do you tell someone, "I just had a dream and God told me to call your number"?

unknown caller on the other side said, "Could you tell me a little about yourself?" And the ECKist said, "Well, I live in Texas and have raised four children. I was a social worker." And then she mentioned that she had lost a son, a grown son in his twenties, to suicide.

The woman said, "It just so happens that I was a dream consultant." She used to live and work in another state. She had had her own radio program, and she gave interviews and often talked with people about their dreams. So she found it very unusual that this ECKist would have gotten her phone number in a dream.

As they talked, the dream consultant asked the ECKist, "What exactly do you want to know?"

The ECKist said, "I want to know if there was any karma on my part that caused my son's suicide." And woman on the other end said, "When you're ready, you will get an answer." The ECKist was thinking she'd like an answer right now. Why else would the Dream Master have given her the phone number of this person who turned out to have been a dream consultant?

The dream consultant explained. When she had given advice on her radio show, people would call back later very upset, because she hadn't given them a very clear, direct interpretation of their dreams. She simply told them, "When you're ready, you will get the answer." But the people were impatient, and they were angry. They wanted their answers right now.

But the ECKist understood. She told the dream consultant, "I understand it's my responsibility. When I'm ready, I will get my answer. I also understand that my son's suicide is entirely his responsibility."

When you're ready, you will get the answer.

She had been afraid to go to sleep at night because of a fear that the Inner Master would give her an answer before she was ready to hear it. And the dream consultant's answer was assurance to her that she had only to wait, and when the time was right—in a week, a month, ten years, whatever it took—the answer would come.

The ECKist asked the dream consultant, "Where can I find your books? Will they be in a regular bookstore?"

"Actually this is the most unusual way that Divine Spirit has ever had someone contact me," the dream consultant said, "so I'll send you the books."

So in this first conversation the ECKist learned that she was not responsible for her son taking his life. And she got assurance that she would find the answers for the karmic involvement when the time was right. Because as the dream consultant had told her, "His suicide affected many people. And if I gave you a direct answer right now, what would you do with the answer? Would you carry the answer to some people who are not ready for it yet?"

The dream consultant also said, "The dream worlds are the real worlds. This world is the dream." And so ended the first phone call.

The second day, another call came. It was from a sales professional. Again the woman said, "I had this dream, and I got your number."

"I don't want to be rude, but I want to remind you this is a long-distance call," the man said.

"Can I call you back?" the ECKist asked. And he agreed. So she called him back.

Again she told about the death of her son, and she explained a little more about having gotten the man's number through a dream. "Can you make a

The dream consultant also said, "The dream worlds are the real worlds. This world is the dream."

connection of any sort in this?" the woman asked.

In a very matter-of-fact voice he said, "Three people died in my family recently. People die." So they talked a little bit more. And after a while he said, "This is all I can do to help you. I think I've been very fair to you." And she agreed that he had been very fair, giving of his time.

When they had hung up, the woman realized that Divine Spirit had given her a message through him too. The message was (1) to be a little bit more careful about financial matters, and (2) not to be so attached to material things, including our loved ones.

It sounds like a paradox, but it isn't.

We have these strong feelings for our loved ones. We've grown used to each other and each other's habits. We may not always be totally happy with each other, because we all have those tough days. But we love the people we're with, and we dearly miss them when it's their time to go.

Soul comes from the inner planes, manifesting here in a baby's body and going through the experiences of life. Then It goes on.

CAN YOU LOVE GOD MORE?

The man had said, "I recently lost three people in my family. People die." He had said it as if it was very natural. Just like in the natural world, the animals understand that they come and go, they come and they go.

And we in Eckankar understand this coming and going of Soul too. Soul comes from the inner planes, manifesting here in a baby's body and going through the experiences of life. Then It goes on. The coming and the going. And the coming repeats again, because this is the journey of Soul. What is the whole purpose? Basically to give a yes answer to the question Can you love God more?

And even when we don't love God, God loves us. God shows this love constantly through Divine Spirit, the ECK.

How God Uses Us

A high-school counselor was assigned to students who were about fourteen to eighteen years old. She had been a teacher for eighteen years and a counselor for twelve. Her job was to help students decide which courses would help them toward a career, perhaps college.

One day she was in her office with a seventeen-year-old girl, a junior. They were trying to get together some kind of course of study for the girl's senior year. They were having an awfully hard time. The high-school counselor sat back in her chair and looked out the window, and she happened to see a dear friend of hers arrive at the school.

Sometimes the friend would drop in just to say hi. So she waved to her friend on the other side of the open window. "I'm busy, but I'll be out there in a minute, and maybe we can talk on the phone later," she said.

"Would you excuse me a moment?" the counselor asked the student. "My friend is outside, and I'd just like to see her for a minute. I'll be right back."

It was OK with the student, because she and the counselor were getting nowhere at this point, trying to figure out which courses she would take for the next year. So the counselor went looking for her friend, but she couldn't find her. She even looked around the parking lot for the van her friend drove. No van. Very puzzled, the counselor came back into the building and went back to the room with the junior who was still waiting to finish the counseling session. The

Even when we don't love God, God loves us. God shows this love constantly through Divine Spirit, the ECK.

counselor apologized again, and they continued to talk. But from that moment on, all the courses fell into place for the junior's schedule for the next year. Suddenly it all went very, very smoothly. Everything just fell together.

So that night after work the high-school counselor called her friend. "I'm really sorry that we missed each other at school. I came out to find you, but you were already gone." And her friend didn't know what she was talking about. She said, "But I wasn't at the school today." In fact, she had been in another part of the state.

It finally dawned on them that the Inner Master had appeared in the form of the counselor's friend.

Both of them are members of Eckankar. It finally dawned on them that the Inner Master had appeared in the form of the counselor's friend. And then the counselor asked, "But why in your form?" "Because," the friend said, "if it had been in the form of the Inner Master, you would have been so startled, you would not have been able to function for the rest of the day." The counselor said, "I can understand that. That would have been a little bit shocking to suddenly see the Mahanta, the Living ECK Master standing outside saying, 'Just dropped in to see you. Don't hurry. Go ahead. Work out the courses with your student.' It would not have worked so well."

This is an explanation of how people appear in different places even though they have no knowledge of having been there. They come either to help someone else or in some way just to be there. Other people say, "But we saw you there. Were you there?" It's Divine Spirit, or sometimes the Inner Master, using the form of this person to come. After all, a form is just form.

Soul goes into a form called a human body. And sometimes the Master creates one that can be used to carry a message of a very important spiritual nature to another person.

DO YOU HAVE TROUBLE LOVING GOD?

Another ECKist had been in Eckankar for twelve years, and for most of the time that she was in ECK she had tried to learn Soul Travel. This basically is a more vivid method of dreaming, although that doesn't do it justice. Soul Travel is moving into a higher state of consciousness. But it also can involve seeing people and places at a distance. This is another version of Soul Travel. But for our purposes right now, it's a more vivid way of dreaming.

This woman had wanted to Soul Travel her whole life. After twelve years, she realized that the foundation to the ECK teachings was love—as it is in all major spiritual teachings. Love, divine love. A long time ago she had heard a saying, "Fear knocked at the door, love answered, and no one was there." This is how she remembered it.

But she couldn't fill herself with God's love.

She had no problem with love for her family, love for the ECK Masters, and love for her friends. That was very easy. But she had a very difficult time when it came to loving God. And she couldn't understand this.

And so, in the dream state the next night, three of the ECK Masters came. One was the Mahanta, Wah Z—my spiritual name on the inner planes. The other two were Rebazar Tarzs and Fubbi Quantz, ECK Masters who have served as the Living ECK Master in years gone by.

Rebazar Tarzs asked her, "Why do you think you have trouble loving God?"

Rebazar Tarzs asked her, "Why do you think you have trouble loving God?"

"God is not what I always thought It was," she said.

To me, that is a profound answer. Even people who think they love God may love themselves more. But to truly love God means a willingness to serve God's creatures. Not the way we think they need to be served, but the way Divine Spirit sees they would best be served.

Rebazar Tarzs said to her, "That's the beginning in understanding God."

Then she asked the Mahanta, "How can I love something like God, something that I can't fathom?" And the Mahanta said, "What do you think you *can* love?" As she thought about it, she realized that she could love the things that God created. She could love her family, she could love her friends, the things in nature, happy occasions. She could love all these things. Maybe someday she would also have the capacity, the fathomless love, that Soul has when It loves God.

When the woman realized that, all the three ECK Masters smiled. Then Fubbi Quantz said, "Love everything, and you love God."

Learning to Love

You give warm love to those who are close to you. You give charity, or goodwill, which is a detached form of love, to those beyond your close circle. Because a human being does not have the capacity to love everyone and everything with warm, total love. We do not have the capacity.

An ECKist was reading in one of the ECK books about the dinosaurs on earth. And reading how after God had created them and saw that this experiment had reached its fulfillment, God brought an end to the experiment. She wondered, *How can God do that? How can God create all these huge dinosaurs and then at some point after millions of years say, "Experiment done, wipe the slate clean, and we'll try a new form of life"?* She had trouble with this. So she asked this question in contemplation one day.

Every time she sat down to contemplate, her Siamese cat would sit in her lap and purr joyously. The woman would shut her eyes, sing the holy name of God, HU, and wait until the Light or the Sound come into her inner vision, into her Spiritual Eye.

And the Inner Master said, "If God had not given Soul the experience of the lower worlds in order to become godlike, you could not receive love from your Siamese cat. And you could not return love to her." God made earth and all the material worlds so that Soul could learn to give and receive love.

For all of you who wonder, *What is the purpose of life? Why are we here?* It is to learn to give and receive God's love.

God made earth and all the material worlds so that Soul could learn to give and receive love.

ECK Worldwide Seminar, Minneapolis, Minnesota, Friday, October 20, 1995

As he was driving along the road, he was thinking, *I need a sign.*

2

ARE YOU LOOKING FOR A SIGN FROM GOD?

When I give a talk, I have prepared notes; but I also try to stay open to images that come through from the ECK, or Divine Spirit. And when an image comes, I speak about it. I try, as well as I can, to put it into words for you.

Some people say that Paul Twitchell, the modern-day founder of Eckankar, was nervous before he gave a talk. I wouldn't say it's nervousness so much as wanting to be open—completely clear and open—for the message of Divine Spirit as it comes through. One needs to step out of his own way.

How to Love Better

Sometimes I'll be giving a talk, speaking the ECK message, and my mind will be thinking of other things. Suddenly I'll lose track of what I'm talking about. The ECK message is coming in, and my mind is going some other place. That's when I have to tell myself, *Time to pay attention and be clear for the message of ECK.* It requires complete attention every moment.

Being onstage is not that much different from how you live your life every day. This is true whether you're an ECKist or just someone who loves truth and is not in Eckankar yet.

It requires having your wits about you at all times. I don't mean this in the ordinary sense—a mental game where you try to outwit life. You can't.

The best we can do, in the highest spiritual sense, is to be open to the directions that Divine Spirit gives to us about how to make our daily lives better. And the lesson is very often how to love better with fewer attachments, with fewer ideas about how some event should go.

The best we can do, in the highest spiritual sense, is to be open to the directions that Divine Spirit gives to us about how to make our daily lives better.

A SIGN FROM GOD

An ECKist had a job, but he was looking for a new job. One day he received a job offer from the Eckankar Spiritual Center.

Is this really what I want to do? he wondered. He went back and forth, he had a lot of doubts.

He was out walking one day when he noticed a branch from a pine tree. On it were a number of pinecones. He realized that the job would provide all kinds of opportunity for him. *That's very good,* he thought, *but I would like a little more confirmation.*

I tell the members of ECK not to make important decisions based solely on a dream. For instance, you have a dream that tells you to undertake a certain project or marry a certain person. Take your time, look it over. Get verification from as many different sources as you can.

One day this man was driving to his job while he was still considering whether or not to work at the ECK Spiritual Center. He went by a different route. As he drove along the road, he was wondering, *Is that job right for me; will I really have a chance for spiritual growth and more understanding? In other words, can I learn more?* He still had a lot of doubts. As he was driving along the road, he was thinking, *I need a sign.*

Suddenly he rounded a corner and saw a big billboard. It said, "If you're looking for a sign from God, this is it."

Before he made his decision, he had asked for confirmation. And he got it.

After he accepted the job, he and his supervisor were talking about the details of his responsibilities, and during a break he went outside for a little walk around the block. He came to four large pine trees, and the trees were just full of pinecones. He realized life was speaking to him through the waking dream — an experience that is just a mundane everyday event, but it translates to a very important spiritual message. Those four trees meant that there was even more growth and opportunity in this new job than he had first imagined.

Whenever we come to a job or a position, we realize that as sure as we arrive there, the day will also come when we go. This coming and going is the nature of life in these worlds.

Sometimes the sign from God comes through us to other people. At the time we are being a vehicle for Divine Spirit, we often don't recognize it. We don't realize why we are speaking in a certain manner, maybe more direct than how we normally speak. Yet we do it. Basically, we are a player on the stage of life, being either a conscious or unconscious vehicle for Divine Spirit.

Sometimes the sign from God comes through us to other people.

WHAT ARE YOUR DREAMS?

Last year there was an ECK seminar in Bogotá, Colombia. Several of the ECKists walked around the city and went to look at historical sites.

As they were walking, some kids came up to them begging for money.

Only one of the ECKists spoke Spanish; he was a young man. As the boys said, "Give us money, give us money," in Spanish, the young man asked them, "What do you want money for?" It surprised them that he spoke Spanish, because they hadn't expected it. Usually tourists didn't; the kids would just hold out their palms, which is a universal sign for begging, and the tourists would put something in them.

But the young man asked, "What do you want the money for?" They said, "We're hungry." He looked at them carefully. One of the boys had on a sweatshirt from a university. So he said to the boy, "What are your dreams?" The three boys just stood there and looked at him. So again he asked, "What are your dreams?" He pointed to the sweatshirt from the university and said, "Are you planning to go and get more education?"

What do you want to be, what do you want to become?

They just looked at him, thinking, *Is he some kind of a lunatic or something? Why doesn't he just give us the money the way everybody else does?* They wanted the money; they didn't want the lecture.

The young man said again, "Your dreams, what are your dreams? What do you want to be, what do you want to become?"

No one had ever asked them that before, and they really didn't know what to say. They stood there looking at him, and finally they said, "Well, we don't know."

"You've got to have dreams," the young ECKist told them. "You can't go begging your whole life, because begging is not living." Then finally the boy with the sweatshirt from the university said, "I want to become a soldier." And the ECKist stood back a moment and thought about it. "That is a dream," he said, "and it's better than no dream at all, but it's a dream of power. It will cause you a lot of trouble; but if that's all you can dream, then be a soldier."

Then he said, "It would be far better if you could dream a dream of love."

With that he bowed to them and rejoined the two ECKists he had been with. They couldn't understand Spanish, so one of them asked, "What was all that about? What did the boys want?" And he said, "They wanted money, but the Mahanta wanted me to give them back their dreams." The Mahanta is the spiritual Master in Eckankar.

Sometime in the future, maybe one of the three boys will remember this incident. Maybe he'll go on to better himself through education or some experience in business or life. Maybe he will overcome poverty, whereas maybe his two companions won't.

He'll tell his story to those who care enough to ask him, "How did you ever become successful?" He'll say, "Once when I was a kid begging on the street, I had a sign from God. This big guy looked at us and asked, 'What are your dreams?' Until that time I had never thought about having a dream."

So sometimes this is how a sign from God comes—through other people. Sometimes it comes through you or me. It doesn't matter. Divine Spirit picks the channel who is the most open at that particular moment. And when the Holy Spirit picks someone to do Its bidding for the spiritual benefit of someone

Divine Spirit picks the channel who is the most open at that particular moment.

else, the Holy Spirit doesn't ask, "Are you a Catholic, Lutheran, ECKist, Jew, Muslim, or Hindu?"

The Holy Spirit doesn't ask. Because divine love doesn't make the distinctions that people do.

SPIRITUAL LAWS

When people first come to ECK, they want to serve God in some way.

When people first come to ECK, they want to serve God in some way. Because service to life is the whole point of Eckankar. It doesn't matter how you serve. But you learn to uplift and make a situation better than it was before, to help people see something, in some way.

A dental hygienist in the Minneapolis area got into Eckankar a number of years ago. Shortly after that she was cleaning the teeth of a patient. Out of the blue the man looks at her and says, "Could you recommend a good book on the spiritual laws?"

This is something dental hygienists run into all the time. They have a little drawer right behind them where they have floss, toothpaste and toothbrushes, and a book of the spiritual laws.

Usually there's nothing worse than a new convert. This woman had just gotten into ECK. So she says, "Right, I have an ECK book for you. If you'll drop by the office tomorrow morning, I'll give it to you."

Bright and early the next morning, as soon as the office opened, the man came back, picked up the book, expressed his thanks, and then disappeared for a couple of months. At his next appointment, the dental hygienist couldn't wait to ask him what had happened. *Giving him a good book like this on the spiritual laws,* she thought, *this ought to make him an ECKist. He's probably been an ECKist all this time.*

"Thank you ever so much for the book; it changed my life," the patient told her. "I found a wonderful

Jewish woman, and we're going to get married. I'm going to become a Jew."

The dental hygienist was wondering, *What book did he read? How do you get people to join Eckankar— give them a book on Judaism? Is there some kind of reversed effort here?* She had some strong opinions about this. *The man doesn't know how to go straight ahead. I give him a book to the shortest direct route, and then he goes off some other direction,* she thought.

But then she realized that Divine Spirit gives to people what they need spiritually, not what we think they need. And as soon as she realized this, she could relax. She could allow her patient a very pleasant time in the chair. You have to be careful about talking politics or religion to your dentists and dental hygienists because you never know what you're going to end up with if you find yourself on the losing end of the argument.

Divine Spirit gives to people what they need spiritually, not what we think they need.

THE REST OF THE STORY

We have a lot of books in Eckankar. The Mahanta Transcripts series has good examples about how Divine Spirit works in the lives of people. I tell the stories, but they're usually not my stories; they're your stories. Sometimes you tell them to me; sometimes you write about them in a letter. Sometimes people will tell me a story, but they're missing some details. So I put the details in. I hope they understand. Because sometimes people don't understand. They've missed details—because, if it was a dream, waking up from the dream state is such a transition that it's hard to remember everything when you come back here.

A dream is simply a memory of an experience in the other worlds. And sometimes these experiences are so unlike the day-to-day reality of the individual that they make absolutely no sense.

I'm not talking about things that are shocking — nightmares, for instance. We find that a lot of people have nightmares, especially youth, because they're remembering past lives. They had a very unpleasant experience in a past life, so it comes back and stays with them as they make the transition into this life.

TRUTH OF REINCARNATION

Children of two and three and four, just at the age when they begin talking, often remember past lives very clearly. If you are curious about their memories—without prying too much—you can ask them the question What did you do when you were big? It's a nice question because it opens up windows, not for the child but usually for the parents. Parents often don't realize and understand the fact of reincarnation, the fact that people do come back again and again.

We develop the quality of divine love. We become more godlike beings.

In a Christian society it's a one-life, onetime thing. You live your life for better or for worse, and then you go. That's it. One time upon the stage of earth, and then never to reappear.

But many people of other religions beside Eckankar do understand and accept the principle of reincarnation. It's a principle of divine love in action. It allows people, you and me, to have a chance to develop the quality of divine love. We do this through the hardships and uncertainties, as well as the joys and the fulfillment, of living. We develop the quality of divine love. We become more godlike beings.

Are you looking for a sign from God?

Moving Sale

An ECKist who used to work at the Eckankar
Spiritual Center has moved quite often in the past
year. Those of you who have moved a lot may find
that you have this unsettled feeling. You feel almost
like an animal that doesn't even have a hole in the
ground to call home. Nothing is where you want it.
The furniture that you enjoyed at the last place was
sold. You hit the road, come to a new town, go to
stores, and try to buy things to fill up your new place
again.

*Those of you
who have
moved a lot
may find that
you have this
unsettled
feeling.*

This is what this ECKist was doing. She and her
husband had moved several times, they had a new
apartment, and she needed lamps.

So she went looking for garage sales, and she
came to a place that was having a moving sale. It
was after five o'clock. The person who was conducting the moving sale had actually started to close, but
when she saw the ECKist she opened the door. "I
really don't have a whole lot of things left," the woman
said, "just a couple of lamps." Exactly what the ECKist
was looking for.

And so the two women went inside, talking about
"the joys of moving"—which to them meant not a
whole lot of joy at all. The ECKist was impressed by
the love, warmth, and understanding that the woman
had about the unsettling experiences of moving.

Out of the blue, the ECKist said, "Have you ever
heard about Eckankar?"

"Why, yes, just this morning."

The coincidence startled this woman. As they
talked, she would occasionally get this far-off look in
her eyes and say, "It's incredible. It's incredible that
I'd hear about Eckankar twice in one day."

That morning she and a friend of hers had been setting up the moving sale. The friend was wondering out loud, "So many things happen in our lives that we don't understand, and it would be nice to know about them." And this woman had said, "I know God has a plan, but sometimes I'd like to know more about it too."

She wanted to know if there was a grand scheme to creation that reached even down to her street, right into her very home. If there was such a divine plan, it would be very nice to know about it because then she could put herself in agreement with it, in harmony with it, and maybe spare herself some hard, unnecessary lessons throughout the day.

This woman's friend suddenly remembered, "I've read a couple of books on Eckankar, and maybe that's something that you might want to explore."

The two friends had parted, and the moving sale lasted the rest of the day. And then at the end of the day here comes the ECKist who happens to ask, "Have you ever heard about Eckankar?"

All of a sudden the circle closes very quickly and tightly: what began in the morning comes to fulfillment in the evening.

Why did this ECKist end up at this particular house? And why did she bring up Eckankar?

The ECKist had also been working at the ECK Spiritual Center and was able to give the woman information—where to get ECK books—which the woman's friend had not been able to do.

You see how quickly Divine Spirit works sometimes.

Why did this ECKist end up at this particular house? And why did she bring up Eckankar? She doesn't usually do that. As she's going around the grocery store, she doesn't usually step up to a person in the produce section and, picking up an apple, ask her, "Oh, by the way, have you heard about Eckankar?" Or if in the post office in line to mail a package, ask one of the postal people, "I'd like to mail this first class, and by the way, have you heard about Eckankar?" It doesn't quite fit. It doesn't quite work. Might be interesting if someone tried it, considering the experience of the woman who heard about Eckankar in the morning and again in the evening. First time she hears that she needs to get some books, and the second time she finds out where to get them.

Sometimes, a sign from God comes through other people.

Are you looking for a sign from God?

THE POWER OF HU

There's a young woman who lives in Africa; she's connected with the national assembly in one of the countries. She got into a relationship with an older man when she was twenty-five. Their relationship began with strong affection for each other. But as time went on, she thought to herself, *Sometime I would like to marry and although this man loves me very much, he's not the one I want to spend the rest of my life with, because he has a very possessive love.*

This man had the feeling that she was thinking of ending the relationship, and he turned to black magic. In Africa the power of black magic is very strong. It is a very real force.

People in Western countries might laugh at this, but if you were ever to get to Africa and someone put a curse on you, you would probably find yourself hard pressed to be very objective about it. All sorts of things can go very, very wrong unless you know about the holy word of God, such as HU. You can sing the word *HU* to open yourself to protection from Divine Spirit.

You can sing the word HU to open yourself to protection from Divine Spirit.

The power of black magic is very strong, and so after the older man began to use black magic on her, the young woman began to have nightmares. She found it very difficult to go to sleep. She was afraid of going to sleep.

The young woman mentioned her nightmares to a friend who happened to be an ECKist. There are many Eckankar members in Africa. And the friend said, "You have to be very, very careful about this practice of mysticism. It can hurt you. But there is a way to protect yourself." Then the ECKist told this young woman about HU and how to sing it. "Tonight when you go to bed, sing HU and trust it with your whole heart. I'll sing it too, when I go to bed."

In her dream that night, the older man started to come at her, and she began to sing HU in the dream world, on the inner planes.

In her dream that night, the older man started to come at her, and she began to sing HU in the dream world, on the inner planes. Suddenly he stopped; he couldn't penetrate the wall of protection that Divine Spirit had provided, and he began to disintegrate and vanished.

As soon as this happened, a band of men came on the scene. They were all in white robes except the leader was in a sky blue robe. And she thought, *Oh, oh. These are some of his friends; they must be black magicians who are going to try to have revenge for what's happened to him.*

So to protect herself from them, she began to sing HU. And to her surprise, they sang HU back.

The man in blue asked her, "Where did you learn about HU?"

"From my neighbor," she told him.

The next morning when she awoke, the young woman went next door to her neighbor and told her the dream. "You've met the Mahanta," the ECKist said. "You've met the Inner Master."

A little while later the young woman had another dream. In this dream she saw the painting of a face. It was painted with gold colors like an eternal face, very pleasant to look at. She tried to hold her attention on it, but gradually it faded away.

The next morning she went back to her neighbor, and she said, "I've seen this face painted in gold." And her neighbor said, "You've had another dream with the Master."

And this time the ECKist gave her the address of the Eckankar Spiritual Center. And the young woman wrote to me, "Please send me more information about ECK." She mentioned that HU has become her magic word. It has given her a strength and purpose that she never realized she had been lacking.

FREEDOM

We sent her information about Eckankar, but it's up to her to do with it what she wants. On this path or any other true path, no one can hold another person.

No one can say, "You've studied ECK now for five or ten years, you'll have to stay, you can't leave." I can't say that. I won't say that. Because to do that is to limit my own freedom. Since this is a path of spiritual freedom, I would be very foolish to do so. And I can't because the spiritual law does not allow me to do so. If someone wants to come to ECK and they have the qualifications—a true desire for truth and for God—then I say, "All right, you may become a student of the ECK teachings." And then through the Eckankar Spiritual Center, the people get whatever information they need to become a member and to learn more about the ECK teachings. Some people just want a book. It doesn't matter.

If someone wants to come to ECK and they have the qualifications—a true desire for truth and for God—then I say, "All right, you may become a student of the ECK teachings."

But after a few months, a year, two years, sometimes even ten, fifteen, or twenty years, something comes along to shake their faith. Then they say, "This is not the teaching I thought it was. I'm leaving."And I say, "OK." It's all the same to me. The sun's still going to come up tomorrow.

It really makes no difference to me if you want to be on the path of ECK or not, because you are in life. Whether you follow the path of ECK, Judaism, the Lutheran faith, Catholicism, or any of the other religions that God has put here for the spiritual upliftment of Souls, it doesn't make any difference to me.

Each religion is a school to fit the states of consciousness of people at a given level.

Each religion is a school to fit the states of consciousness of people at a given level. Those people go to that school until they have finished there too.

But whenever anyone leaves any group with anger—whether it's Catholic, Lutheran, Episcopal, Eckankar, or whatever—they still have a lot to learn about divine love. And they will learn it somewhere farther down the road.

FIRST CAUSE

Divine Spirit will bring them to exactly the right place, to exactly the place they belong. And there they will continue their education about the great cause of life. About God, about the first cause.

The first cause is God. And everything that emanates from the Godhead is first cause too. Such as Its voice, the Holy Spirit, and divine love, which is the essence of the message of the Holy Spirit to Souls in all worlds.

Are you looking for a sign from God?

ARE YOU HAVING SPIRITUAL EXPERIENCES?

When people first come to Eckankar, they are accepted as members. But they are not expected to make a commitment to Divine Spirit and this path until after two years. At this time they can request the Second Initiation. If the person makes the request, a Second Initiation form is sent; it's on pink paper, so it's often called a pink slip. It's an invitation to the individual: at this time you may embrace the teachings of ECK should you desire to do so.

There are certain spiritual disciplines that I ask of those who become Second Initiates—and they're very simple. I ask you to keep a dream journal and write monthly initiate reports. You don't have to mail the reports necessarily. An initiate report is a review for yourself of what has happened in your life in the past month. It's for your good, for your benefit.

An initiate report is a review for yourself of what has happened in your life in the past month. It's for your good, for your benefit.

I have heard people complain to me, "I'm just not having any spiritual experiences." And yet the same people have just told me, within the past year, about two or three outstanding Soul Travel or dream experiences. At the time they understood perfectly the significance of the experience and they were so grateful. But the human mind has a habit of forgetfulness.

Three or four months go by, and they don't remember anything. Then they say, "Well, I'm not having any experiences in ECK at all, nor have I ever." I remember, they forget. This is why I say, it would be nice if you wrote these things down. It would save me a lot of correspondence.

DREAM JOURNAL

An ECKist from Nigeria had become a member of ECK. And after he had been a member for two years, he took the Second Initiation.

He went to a distant city to go to an ECK seminar, and when it was over he got a ride halfway back to his home city with some other ECKists. At the midway point where they lived, he was going to get a cab for the rest of the journey. So he said good-bye to his friends and went over to the cabstand. Because it was such a long distance the cabdriver usually waited until the cab was full; this ECKist happened to be the last passenger.

As the ECKist reached for his wallet just to make sure that he could pay when he got home, he discovered that his wallet was gone. He panicked, of course.

He told the cabdriver, "Take me to my hometown, and I'll pay you there." The cabdriver wasn't so sure about this arrangement. Should he trust this guy? It was a long cab ride. As the cabdriver was thinking about it, this man was feeling more and more distressed—no wallet, no money, no keys, no ECK ID card. How was he going to get home?

Suddenly one of the other passengers says, "That's OK, I'll pay his fare." And so the ECKist thanks him very kindly. He says, "I'll pay you back as soon as we get to my hometown." The other man says, "It's not necessary." And when he wouldn't accept payment, the ECKist suddenly got this feeling that the Mahanta, the Living ECK Master had a message for him. The spiritual leader of ECK was trying to get an important lesson across to him. So he's listening very carefully now and trying to figure it out.

When he arrived home, he wanted to pay the man back. But it was Sunday, and the banks are closed on Sunday in that town, so he didn't have any money. But just as he was wondering what to do, a man came to the door. This man represented a former client for

The spiritual leader of ECK was trying to get an important lesson across to him. So he's listening very carefully now and trying to figure it out.

whom this ECKist had done some consulting work. And the man handed the ECKist a large sum of money. So now the ECKist had money to pay the man in the cab.

So the ECKist has his money, but he doesn't have his key. He's a teacher at a large university there. He needed to get into his office, and the keys he had lost were his only set. Usually he never took these keys along on trips, but this time he had forgotten. And so now he was locked out of his office. He wonders what to do.

That night he has a dream, and in it the Inner Master came to him and began speaking with him.

"What about your dream journal?" the Inner Master says.

The ECKist thinks a minute. "I did buy one, and I was going to start recording my dreams right after the Second Initiation, but I forgot."

He had had some very good dream experiences. He now remembered that in one dream the Inner Master had warned him that some people who were going to enter into a business venture with him were dishonest. He saw this, he was able to protect himself, and he saved himself a lot of money. He could have written that in his dream journal, but he forgot.

Then the Master said, "What about your initiate report? Where is this report that you should be writing for your own benefit each month? Even if you don't mail it, just write it."

"I forgot," said the ECKist.

The Master then used a very interesting term: "Indiscipline." Not a "lack of discipline," but "indiscipline." "The lost wallet and keys are a waking dream of locking yourself out of the spiritual worlds 'by indiscipline,'" the Inner Master said. "You have to

"The lost wallet and keys are a waking dream of locking yourself out of the spiritual worlds 'by indiscipline,'" the Inner Master said.

make changes if you want to open up your spiritual life."

Shortly after that this ECKist had a dream, and in it he met his friend who lives in the city where the ECK seminar was held. His friend said in the dream, "I found your wallet, and I'll send it to you with a note."

But the next morning when the ECKist woke up, he didn't trust this dream. An acquaintance was going to be going to that city, so he gave him a note for his friend, saying, "If you find my wallet, please send it back."

The next day his wallet arrived, and in it were the keys and his ECK ID. Everything was back in order.

The ECKist realized that his wallet hadn't really been lost at all. It was just in someone else's keeping. He realized that this whole situation had been given to him to help him. It was a sign from God, to help him move along in his own spiritual life.

It was a sign from God, to help him move along in his own spiritual life.

GOD'S PERFECT PLAN

An ECKist in Germany was also looking for a sign from God. She was having trouble trying to figure out how to conduct her life so as to be the most beneficial.

About this time, she read a biography of an American doctor who had been a young man at the end of World War II. He was sent to Germany after the war and worked in one of the concentration camps that had been freed by the Allies. His job was to take care of the ex-prisoners who were ill.

Many of his patients were in very poor shape, too sick to even travel from the concentration camp. His job was to get them better so that they could travel.

As the doctor examined the former prisoners he saw one man who was the picture of health: his eyes were shining, there was strength in them, and he looked like a fountain of water in the desert. And he had the respect of all the other former prisoners. *This guy probably just got here,* the doctor thought. *He was probably one of the last people to come to the concentration camp, that's why he looks so good.*

So he got in a conversation with him. It turns out the man was a lawyer, and he had been in the camp since 1939, almost from the beginning. And yet he survived, strong and in good health. The American doctor asked him how he had come through all this with such flying colors.

And the lawyer told his story.

Back in 1939 he had been married. He had two daughters and three sons. When the Nazis came, they dragged him and his family out into the street. They shot his wife and children. And he begged them to let him go with them too. But because he spoke several languages, the Nazis said he would be of use to them in the concentration camp.

And right there on the street, with his family lying dead at his feet, he made a decision. He said, "Will I go the path of hate or the path of love?" As a lawyer he had seen too much of the destructive power of hate. How people who hated so much went to the courts and destroyed themselves. And this man, standing there with his life literally in ruins about him, chose to go the path of love. For this reason, he had survived six years in perhaps the most hellish place on earth.

He said, "Will I go the path of hate or the path of love?"

When the German ECKist read this biography, she realized that she had to make peace with herself. She had to accept life as God's perfect plan. To her, this book was a sign from God.

There are many different ways a sign from God may come—through books, through people, through dreams. Because God is speaking at all times through the Holy Spirit. And It's speaking with the divine voice of love.

Are you looking for a sign from God?

A SPIRITUAL HEALING

God is speaking at all times through the Holy Spirit. And It's speaking with the divine voice of love.

A woman in Jamaica had lost her husband; he was only thirty-eight. They had two children. Right after the tragedy occurred that took her husband's life, she was wondering how was she going to support her children.

As she was trying to figure out how to make a living for her children, she discovered something very interesting. Some people were very kind and thoughtful and helped her in every way possible during this time. On the other hand, some of her acquaintances were envious and jealous and angry, and during this darkest hour they tried to take away what little she had. She wondered, *What makes people like that? Why would some people try to cheat her at this time?*

She looked for answers through her church, but she couldn't get any.

One day a business client told her about HU and loaned her an ECK book. Shortly after reading the ECK book, she had a dream.

In the dream the Inner Master came to her, and he was speaking to her, trying to tell her something. But she couldn't hear him. He could see that she couldn't hear the spiritual words he was saying to her, so he put his hand over her heart. She had been filled with grief and fear and heartache, but when he put his hand over her heart she suddenly felt such great love, warmth, and kindness.

When she woke the next morning, it was as if some awful burden had lifted from her.

A few days later, she ran into her brother. "What happened to you?" he said.

"Why, what do you mean?"

And he said, "You look so different. You're bright and cheerful." It was at this point that she recognized the miracle that had happened in her life. The Mahanta, the Living ECK Master had given her a healing in her dream, when he put his hand over her heart.

If you are looking for a sign from God, look no farther than within arm's reach. Signs from God are all around; open your eyes to see them. May the blessings be.

If you are looking for a sign from God, look no farther than within arm's reach.

ECK Worldwide Seminar, Minneapolis, Minnesota, Saturday, October 21, 1995

Ringo loved children, and he'd lie at the back of the room, thumping his tail on the floor, enjoying the school year, picking up what he could about ABCs and one plus one.

3

The Most Secret Part of Yourself

Thirty years have passed since Paul Twitchell brought out the teachings of ECK. We generally think in terms of the founders of organizations as being stuffy and rigid. And perhaps that's often so.

But when Paul was young, he was somewhat of a rebel; he had his own mind. One time when he was about four years old, his grandmother gave him a dollar; and a dollar in the early 1900s was worth a lot more than it is now. She said to him, "Paul, you can spend this anyway you want."

Peanuts

So he went down the street to the store. He liked shelled peanuts. He went into the store, he put his dollar down, and he said to the man, "I want a dollar's worth of shelled peanuts." Of course, a dollar would buy a shopping bag full of peanuts. But being four, he didn't know. He just wanted a dollar's worth of shelled peanuts.

The man tried to reason with him. "Why don't you spend ten cents on peanuts, save the other ninety cents, and come back for more later on?"

No, Paul wanted one dollar's worth of shelled peanuts. The man wouldn't give it to him.

So Paul went to the phone and called his mother, and he said, "I want to buy some peanuts. Will you tell the man to sell them to me?"

Paul didn't tell his mother that he wanted a dollar's worth of peanuts, he just said he wanted to buy peanuts and the man wouldn't sell them. Those of you who are parents know this trick. So his mother talked to the grocery clerk and said, "Give him what he wants." After all, she reasoned, what can go wrong? So the grocer said, "OK." He filled a huge bag. But it was too big; Paul couldn't carry the bag home.

So Paul walked home, got his little wagon, and came back to the store. The grocer very kindly packed the bag on Paul's little wagon and braced it very carefully. Paul walked home with his one dollar's worth of shelled peanuts.

There was a five-week supply, he said. For an adult. So for five weeks his mother was grinding up peanuts into peanut butter, and they were having peanuts every meal. He ate a lot of peanuts, but he never lost his taste for them even after that.

He started out a rebel. He had his own mind about things. He liked to do things for a little while. Then after he'd done them for a bit and he had grown tired of them, he'd want to do something else. He looked here, there, and everywhere.

Paul said how very important it was for children to have a pet of some kind—if at all possible.

POWER OF PETS

Paul said how very important it was for children to have a pet of some kind—if at all possible. Today it's a little bit harder in some circumstances. So many people live in small apartments, and then they have problems with the landlords. But sometimes you don't have to own the pet; if you love pets they'll come to your door. And they'll probably be a neighbor's pet. So you get all the advantages of a pet without having to worry about it.

At least I've found that so. Usually some animal comes and stands at the door. "Hi, glad you're here," they'll say. Cats always let you know it's a privilege to pet them. Dogs are so servile and so loving. They'll say, "I'm so glad you're here." But cats say, "Aren't you glad I'm here?"

Dogs are so servile and so loving. They'll say, "I'm so glad you're here." But cats say, "Aren't you glad I'm here?"

When my wife and I are driving or walking down the street, we'll see an owner come along with a dog or two or more. And there is such a resemblance. You can look at them and say, "Do you think they're of the same family?" Man and beast, or beast and the high form of life called dog. Human nature being what it is. I ask my wife sometimes, "I wonder how that dog picked its owner, because they look so much alike. How do they do it?"

A woman had lost her cat; the cat had run away. So the woman would go down to the animal shelter every day to see if her cat had been brought in. One day she saw this beautiful golden-white cat waving at her. Cats are not stupid. And so, of course, she took that cat home. What else can you do?

Paul Twitchell took his dog, Ringo, to school when he was in first grade. Paul and Ringo were very close friends.

Ringo was a black dog, with white legs, who had a splash of white across his face and one black eye. The dog was very patient and very good. Paul said later that the teacher began to give Ringo a report card too—always on behavior, because that's the only thing the teacher could grade the dog on. Ringo always got an *A*. Paul didn't say what he got.

The teacher even began to write little notes on the dog's report card like, "Never speaks unless spoken to, and doesn't smell like a dog." And Paul said that was true, Ringo never smelled like a dog.

Ringo was very quiet and happy. He loved children, and he'd lie at the back of the room, thumping his tail on the floor, enjoying the school year, picking up what he could about ABCs and one plus one. Ringo went to school until the sixth grade when Paul graduated. The junior high school wouldn't allow dogs, so that was the end of Ringo's education. But that was OK; Ringo was getting old. He had put in enough years of his life getting an education, and he was wondering what was he going to do with this education anyway. So mostly he stayed at home from that time on and just enjoyed sleeping through the rest of his years.

A pet gives complete attention and devotion to the owner. Some people need this, especially children.

DO ANIMALS FEEL LOVE?

Paul said it was very important for him to have a pet when he was young, because a pet gives complete attention and devotion to the owner. Some people need this, especially children.

At different stages in our life we find it very, very helpful that Divine Spirit has sent such a good friend, a dog or a cat or a parakeet, even a goldfish. Something to show the divine love that is so necessary for all beings.

A scientist would ask, Do animals feel love? Can they give love? I suppose they'll believe that this is possible once someone does a scientific test. Once some study has said, "There seems to be correlation between pet A and owner A, and pet B and owner B. There seems to be some kind of an attraction and some kind of correlation of interchanging energies."

Basically, if you have a pet, love the pet.

A pet teaches children how to love, or at least it doesn't shut off the loving which is normal and natural for children. It gives them an outlet. It's a very important foundation for the future.

HEART OF LOVE

The most secret part of yourself is the heart of love.

Paul spoke of getting to the most secret part of yourself through contemplation, through the Spiritual Exercises of ECK. Contemplation is a conversation with the most secret, most genuine, and most mysterious part of yourself. And Paul wondered why anyone who knew about the Spiritual Exercises of ECK wouldn't do them.

The most secret part of yourself is the heart of love.

He said that the ECK chelas have the greatest gift that life can give them, a way to come into contact with this mysterious part, which is the secret to life itself. Yet they won't do the spiritual exercises. He found this very, very hard to understand.

I mention this to give you an insight into how very important the spiritual exercises are. They help you discover that inner, mysterious part of yourself.

We speak about dreams; we speak about Soul Travel, about the ECK-Vidya, which is the ancient science of prophecy, and all the different miracles of upliftment that we feel in times of distress or stress.

Help is so close, help is so near. All you have to do is do your part. All you have to do is take the key and put it in the door of your heart, and the Mahanta will turn the key and open the door.

And the door opens, of course, to God's love — infinite, boundless, refreshing love, like a fountain in the desert.

DREAMS ARE A KEY

Dreams are one key to help us understand this secret part of ourselves.

A secretary was working with one of the major studios in California. She was a very good secretary. The company assigned her to a different executive. One of her coworkers said to her, "Good luck. He's gone through twelve secretaries in a year." He was one of those unreasonable people, one of the curses that make people say, "What a way to go through life, and he's my boss."

But she had been at this particular studio for three years, and she knew the ways of the company. She knew that she could help her boss and protect him from the company so that he wouldn't step over the line. She knew how things were done, and she was very proud of that.

He was like a bad child. He had his tantrums, and he always wanted to have his way. But they got along tolerably well.

Time went on, and after she had been assigned to him for a month, she was asked to be a temporary secretary somewhere else for a week. And as the week came closer, she tried to help him prepare, trying at all times to be a clear, open channel for Divine Spirit. In other words, just to serve this rather impossible man, despite himself.

But one day just before she was to go on this one-week transfer to another job, things got to the breaking point for her. He was acting as though she didn't know her job at all. She knew it very well. But he just didn't appreciate her. "This is as much as I can take," she said. And she left the room and shut the door.

But she realized that it was a mistake because somewhere in her own past she had had problems with that sort of confrontation. An extreme confrontation would come up, and she would always fly off in anger. She realized it hurt her spiritually. She said somehow she had to get through the natural cycle with this man.

So she went back in the room and apologized, and they talked about it and smoothed things out. So the time came for her to go on the weeklong assignment. And he said, "Well, at the end of that time, I would like you to come back." She agreed to think about it and let him know. The man had gone through twelve secretaries in a year, and after being with him for a month, she felt she had put in her time. She would think about it.

She took the temporary job, and while she was away, she was offered a permanent job, which was very good for her, considering these circumstances. She took it.

She called her former boss and said she wouldn't be coming back. He should find someone else. Then, so he would still have control, he said, "Yes, you won't be coming back to this job." She had already left; she had another job. But some people need to be in control every minute. And so he said, "You won't be needed." As if somehow that was going to make a difference. He was going to be going through more temporary secretaries, and she had a permanent job.

All this time she had been very curious: What is the lesson behind this? What was she supposed to be learning spiritually from this experience with this unreasonable boss?

She remembered another confrontation they had had just before she left on the week's vacation from

All this time she had been very curious: What is the lesson behind this?

him. He was scolding her about one thing or another, and she was standing there with a frozen smile pasted on her face. Suddenly she remembered something from one of the ECK books: If you're ever in a bad situation, imagine the presence of the Mahanta beside you and sing HU.

So as she stood there taking this storm of anger from her boss, she visualized the Mahanta, the Living ECK Master beside her. She began to sing HU quietly, and she felt this warm fountain of love flowing into her.

The smile on her face—instead of being painted on artificially—became genuine. She could see the play of karma, and it didn't bother her. She could appreciate this person as Soul, having helped her with her own anger and her own inability to see what spiritual lesson was here for her.

Not long after she left, she had a dream. It showed her more of why she had been through this situation.

In the dream she was in a room working on a newsletter. In the door walked a lion. The lion was about to spring and attack her, so she shut her eyes and began to sing HU, again imagining the Mahanta beside her. This turned the lion in her dream from a vicious and angry beast into a loving animal of great strength. The lion left her alone.

When she woke up, she realized that she had finished the cycle of karma with her boss.

Incidentally, the studio she worked for had recently released the animated film *The Lion King*.

"I FOLLOW THE MAHANTA"

A flight attendant went to the ECK Worldwide Seminar in Atlanta one year. Two weeks after the seminar, her arm suddenly went limp. It was very

If you're ever in a bad situation, imagine the presence of the Mahanta beside you and sing HU.

painful, and she couldn't use it. This made her work as a flight attendant very difficult.

She was looking through her memory banks trying to remember how she had hurt her arm. Maybe it was helping a passenger lift one of those bloated suitcases into one of the overhead storage bins. She was trying to think, where could she have hurt her arm? Nothing came to mind. She couldn't think of any one instance that might have injured her arm and caused such extreme pain.

So while she was wondering about this, she got a call from an old friend. They had been in another religious group previously, but then the ECKist had found the teachings of Eckankar. The friend said that their former teacher in the other religion had recently died.

The friend went on and on: What a wonderful sweet person this teacher had been!

The ECKist knew there were two sides to the story. The former teacher had taught her for seventeen years, and they had been very close friends at one time. While the teacher was still alive, the ECKist thought, *I'll take her a couple of ECK books. This would be a perfect gift, and maybe she can find some truth in there for herself.*

> While the teacher was still alive, the ECKist thought, I'll take her a couple of ECK books. This would be a perfect gift, and maybe she can find some truth in there for herself.

The ECKist was working for an airline, and she had a ticket, so she flew to the city in California where this woman lived. And as soon as she got there, the woman said, "You can't leave our teachings."

"Why not?" asked the ECKist.

"Because once you've been taught these teachings, these teachings are with you forever." Which may be true, but that doesn't mean you have to be a part of any organization. For the next hour or two, the ECKist had to listen to this angry scolding about how she could not leave. She was given all the dogma of this organization because the teacher was trying to hold her.

When they finally parted that day, the ECKist felt very sad. She couldn't understand why this had happened. It stayed with her for a long time. Then her friend called and said the teacher had died.

Several days later, the ECKist remembered a dream that revealed this most secret part of herself at a level that she hadn't suspected.

Right after the former teacher had died, she had made one last attempt to bring the ECKist back to her religious teaching. In the dream she reached through the veil and grabbed at the ECKist's shoulder and pulled. The ECKist said, "What are you doing?" The woman replied, "You belong in this teaching. I need you."

The ECKist said, "But I follow the Mahanta."

Suddenly the Mahanta appeared beside her, and her old teacher finally understood that she could not hang on to someone who was searching for truth.

Spiritual law prohibits anyone, including myself, from putting a hold on a seeker of truth.

Some teachers try to hang on to their students, but I always let them go. I just say, "OK, you've been in ECK awhile, and you want to go, that's fine." I say, "Sure." Because their life is their experience. And if they want to go somewhere else, it is their absolute right to do so. Spiritual law prohibits anyone, including myself, from putting a hold on a seeker of truth.

But this teacher had tried, and the ECKist now realized this was why her arm had been hurting her. She found out later her shoulder had been dislocated, and she had to go to a chiropractor for treatment. Slowly she got the use of her arm back.

The dream state is a tool that the Mahanta uses

to teach you about some essential spiritual point that you need to know. She learned that she had the freedom to go where she wanted to spiritually and that no teacher from the past or present could hold her, lay any claim to any part of her, including her arm.

LEARNING THROUGH GIVING

Other times the most secret part of yourself reveals itself not through a dream or through some inner manifestation, but through the loving service that you give to others.

A family had a business, and it was doing very well. It gave them a car and a nice home. But with the recession the business went bankrupt. And the family fell into hard times. For the first time there was no money coming in, and they were living off their credit cards to buy food and other necessities, just doing the best they could.

Some of the things the family had bought years ago, like their furniture, were getting a little bit run down, but they had never expected the business to fail. Some of these things needed replacing, but all the money was going toward food.

The mother of the family began feeling a little sorry for herself and becoming despondent. And then she remembered hearing or reading somewhere in the ECK works that if you want to overcome despondency, try giving of yourself to others.

At her children's school there was a social worker. The social worker was trying to help this family, but the mother said, "We'll be OK, but Christmas is coming. Are there any families that I could help?"

The social worker was a little surprised to hear someone from a family who had just lost its business offer to do something for someone else. "Yes, there

Other times the most secret part of yourself reveals itself through the loving service that you give to others.

are ten families in this area that won't have any presents or a special meal at Christmas," the social worker told the mother. So the ECKist began asking around among her friends, gathering toys and food donations. One of her friends, another ECKist, donated ten turkeys. And by the time Christmas came, she had enough presents and food for the ten families.

She had, in a way, given perhaps ten times of herself. But she never thought about that. She did notice that her despondency had lifted, and she was grateful for the healing.

After their business failed, her husband had gotten a job at an apartment complex. And not long after the wife had finished gathering all the Christmas gifts for the ten families, her husband called her and said that one of the tenants at the complex had left, and they had inherited everything left in the apartment. There was a television set and car phone and a stereo — things they needed, all in good condition.

As we're learning about the most secret part of ourselves, we try different spiritual techniques and exercises.

Divine Spirit usually rewards us in more intangible ways, but this time the gifts were very real, the woman realized.

CONNECT WITH SPIRIT

As we're learning about the most secret part of ourselves, we try different spiritual techniques and exercises. We're using our creativity to learn how to work with Divine Spirit, how to come into harmony with life around us.

One ECKist wrote a whole bunch of notes on little cards, all kinds of things like "self is Soul." They were usually neutral themes of one kind or another so that Divine Spirit would have a chance to work with her. She put these little cards facedown in a basket. Every day she would reach in the basket, swish all the little cards around, pick out one, and turn it face up. For the rest of the day she would be very open to any experience that came along the lines of what she had read on the card.

One of the cards was "connect with Spirit." The day she picked that card, she had to go to the bank. There was a customer ahead of her at the teller's window. When the teller had finished with that customer, the customer started to leave. The ECKist came up to the teller's window and asked for the balance on her account. When he heard these words, all of a sudden the teller got this puzzled look on his face. He had forgotten something.

Every little thing in life, every little incident has some spiritual connection.

"Excuse me, I forgot to give that customer the balance on his account," he said to the ECKist.

He ran out of the bank, caught up with the customer, and brought him back to the window, and they finished their business. And after he was finished, the teller served the ECKist.

The ECKist realized that sometimes Divine Spirit works through us as channels—balancing an account. When she said those words to the teller, he remembered that he hadn't finished serving the previous customer.

Some of you will ask, "What's so spiritual about a teller helping someone at a bank window?"

Every little thing in life, every little incident has some spiritual connection. She realized that this was one of those "connect with Spirit" incidents or events.

Another time one of her office friends was leaving, and they had said their good-byes. She had tried to arrange to go out for coffee with this friend, but there never was time. She had so many things to do before she left.

But now the day was close when she would be gone. The woman was driving past her friend's home on the way to have her morning break. *I wonder if she's home and if she has time to come out with me,* she thought. She spent a few minutes deliberating and decided to stop. She drove into the driveway just as her friend was packing some things in her car. "Hey, would you like to come and have coffee?" she asked. "Sure, I'd love to," the friend said.

As they sat over their coffee, they were telling stories about work. And it gradually came out that the friend had fears about leaving her job and going out into the great unknown. She had many fears about the future. But they laughed and had a good time recalling some of the funny things that had happened to them at work. By the time they left the restaurant, the woman felt much better about her move. And the ECKist felt good that she had taken the time to stop and ask her friend to have coffee.

By the time they left the restaurant, the woman felt much better about her move. And the ECKist felt good that she had taken the time to stop and ask her friend to have coffee.

Golden Thread

Another card that she used as a spiritual exercise was "self as Soul." She was to give an introductory talk on Eckankar, and when she arrived at the meeting room, some people were already there. She walked into the room, and one person called out to her, "Hi, how are you doing?" The ECKist who was to give the lecture couldn't quite remember the woman's name; her face was familiar, but she couldn't remember her name.

The two women talked, and the other woman said, "Actually, I only know your name because it's on the program. You look so familiar to me, but I don't remember where we've met before." These two women were chatting like old friends, even though they'd never met each other.

Yogi Berra once said, "It was déjà vu all over again." He was with the New York Yankees baseball team, and he had this way of mangling the simplest statement. But there was also truth in what he said, sometimes so much so that people just stopped and looked at him, because in some odd sort of way it did make sense.

This woman experienced a sense of déjà vu with the person at the introductory talk. She never found out where this acquaintance had formed, but she realized that in any event, no matter how insignificant, there was a golden thread running through it. And the golden thread is the divine love of the Holy Spirit that comes directly from on high, from God.

CREATIVE SPARK OF GOD

A student of ECK from Germany was working in the dream state with the spiritual exercises. At one particular point in his spiritual unfoldment he came to the experience where you can go through walls if you wish, in the dream state. Sometimes you can do this during Soul Travel too, which is a most direct and vivid experience.

Soul Travel is a most direct and vivid experience.

It's like being a ghost, being able to enter a room without bothering to swing the door open. You just go through the wall. Carpenters have one perspective on buildings. They know what's inside the wall, what's inside the Sheetrock, underneath the paint and the spackling. If you have experiences of this nature, it gives you a whole different perspective on buildings.

But if you are able to go outside the human consciousness, to go in Soul form and perhaps see the earth—sometimes from a platform out in space—

you never look at things the same way again. You look at things a little bit different than most people. It's not like the pictures television cameras send back to earth; the experience in the Soul body is entirely different, it's totally alive.

And in a more mundane realm of travel, just being loose in your own home, a person can find himself walking through the kitchen wall to the living room. It is different. It is kind of fun. As long as you keep your attention on the Holy Spirit. But you also have to fill your heart with love, with divine love, as this experience comes.

Usually, it's the Mahanta that will give you an experience such as this. This is by no means the only experience you may have; there are many more. Each will give you a broader viewpoint about life and its infinite possibilities and the power of creativity.

Because, after all, this is everything that Soul is about. Soul is a spark of God. And we always have to say, too, that It is a creative spark of God.

When we have troubles and problems here on earth, it's easy to put out our hand like a little beggar boy and say, "Put something there because I want something." It's a form of creativity, begging, but it's not a very high form. There's an art to it, but it's not the best use of Soul's creativity. There are other ways to draw upon the infinite abundance of life without having to grovel in the dirt like a beggar and act like a slave.

There are ways to recognize your Godhood, the Godness within you. To open yourself to help from the dream state, from the Mahanta. To find out how to take care of yourself better.

Usually this means letting go of some of your old ideas of who and what you are.

Soul is a spark of God. And we always have to say, too, that It is a creative spark of God.

Sometimes people have a very low opinion of themselves, and so they never achieve much in life. No surprise. Like begets like. But when you develop a better opinion of yourself, you find that doors open. One of the reasons that the Inner Master sometimes gives people the experience of walking through walls is so that they can learn that Soul can walk through walls.

HEART LIKE BUTTER

A spiritual student from Germany used a spiritual technique to help him with problems in daily life. One day he had to return something to a store. As he thought about the return, he felt that the salesman wasn't going to want to take back the item. In his mind's eye he could see a confrontation: the salesman would say, "I'm sorry, I can't take that back; you cannot return it." They would have words. And he might even leave the store with his purchase still on the counter as a sign of protest.

But instead of following this direction, he said, "I will leave my heart soft, like warm butter." Because when his heart was just like warm butter, he found in the dream state he could pass right through the walls.

As soon as he became fearful, his heart turned cold. You know what happens to butter when it turns cold; it gets very firm like a brick.

So he went to the store, faced the clerk, and held in his mind's eye this image of melting butter, saying to himself, *My heart is like melting butter.* And it worked.

Of course, men have more of a problem returning things. They think, *I don't know if I can return this or not.* I was that way until I watched my wife at

One of the reasons that the Inner Master sometimes gives people the experience of walking through walls is so that they can learn that Soul can walk through walls.

work. She's very good at it; most women are better
at this sort of thing than men. Women say, "I bought
it, I'm going to take it back." The clerk says, "You can't
bring it back." "Yes, I can; here it is," they say. "It's
in good shape; I didn't damage it. What's the matter?
This should be one of the simpler things in your day."

For men, one of the harder things in their day
is facing the clerk and admitting they made a mistake in buying something. In my experience, women
don't care. They say, "Sure, we make mistakes; we
all make mistakes, hundreds of times a day. Who
cares? Take it back." They take it back. No problem.

I'm generalizing about my experience with men
and women, and my experience as a man watching
my wife return things. She has such a very nice,
natural way of doing it; I'm picking up some pointers.

They say you can't teach an old dog new tricks,
but if you want to learn, you can learn.

*They say
you can't teach
an old dog
new tricks, but
if you want to
learn, you
can learn.*

THE RIGHT WAY TO LIVE

Many people volunteer in one way or another at
ECK seminars, and for this I would like to thank you.
I know of a meeting-room supervisor who likes to
serve at ECK seminars; he likes to make things easier
for the people who are coming to the seminar. As one
of his jobs, he had to set up one of the meeting rooms.

He got up about five o'clock in the morning to be
on site by 5:30. He figured it would take him an hour
to set up the room he was responsible for. As he began
to set it up, another ECKist came by.

"Hey, do you want some help?" the other ECKist
asked. He said, "Sure." So they both worked at it, and
twenty minutes later they finished what otherwise
would have been an hour's work for one person.

They got talking, and one of the ECKists said,

"Life has so many unknown elements to it, it would really be nice to sometimes know how to work with them. It would be good to know God's plan. It would be really nice to know how the divine law works."

One of the spiritual laws is the Law of Economy. And after they finished their little talk, the meeting supervisor had to go up to the floor above and take care of a room up there, to make sure everything was in order for the meeting that was to be held there in a few minutes. As he was going up the escalator, he saw one of the hotel people whose job was to clean the escalator.

One of the spiritual laws is the Law of Economy.

The cleaning man got on the escalator, and he sat down on a step with a rag in each hand. One rag had polish on it. With that rag he polished the bright metal base of the escalator. He just held the polishing rag in one hand and the buffing rag in the other, and he rode the elevator up, seated, cleaning all the way.

Now that is a good use of his energy, thought the ECKist.

Instead of turning off the escalator, polishing the escalator one step at a time very slowly, and putting an escalator out of business for all the people in the hotel, this guy just sat down and polished the metal as he went up. And he probably polished the metal on the other escalator on his way down.

The ECKist realized that there is a right way to live life, and the right way is to go in harmony with life.

Let life carry you like the escalator carried the cleaning man. And then, wherever life takes you, just put out one hand with the polishing rag and the other hand with the buffing rag, and make life around you as pretty and as good as you can.

If you can do this, then you are living the spiritual

I am always with you and my love is with you all the time, in every place.

life. And you are in harmony with Divine Spirit.

As you travel home, know that I am always with you and my love is with you all the time, in every place.

ECK Worldwide Seminar, Minneapolis, Minnesota, Sunday, October 22, 1995

You need a coat. You probably don't need twenty coats; maybe that's when you're crossing the line.

4
MASTER YOUR SPIRITUAL DESTINY

*E*ach of you has a spiritual purpose for coming into this lifetime. I would say that probably 1 percent of the population is aware of that. Most people do not realize they have come to earth with a spiritual purpose. They just think they're here: *I'm here; I don't know why. Bad luck, I guess.*

One morning I woke up at four, and things came through that should be mentioned in this talk. Details like the five passions of the mind and the five virtues. I didn't want to talk about this, because after people have been in ECK awhile they've heard a lot about the five passions. They hear a speaker start to talk about them, and their eyes glaze over and their ears fill with wax. From that point the speaker is pretty much in his own little bubble, and the audience is pretty much in its own little world, and that goes on until he finishes. So I thought, *I won't touch it at all.* But then I thought, *I'll touch it just a little bit—just mention it.*

YOU ARE HERE FOR A PURPOSE

To master your spiritual destiny, you at least have to be aware of what the five passions of the mind are.

Most people do not realize they have come to earth with a spiritual purpose.

The purpose of the spiritual path of ECK—through the dream state and the outer teachings, the discourses and so on—is to give you an idea of how to approach this whole problem: how to become a more spiritual being and master your spiritual destiny.

This is the big challenge you have in this lifetime. But this challenge is covered up with a whole lot of little challenges—like the children screaming when you're trying to get dinner ready and you've had a hard day at work. Little things like this get in the way. They cloak, or hide, the fact that you have a spiritual destiny, that you came here for a purpose.

So the first thing you have to do is realize that you are here for a purpose. And, secondly, discover what you are going to do about it.

FIVE PASSIONS OF THE MIND

Five things that very strongly stand in the way are the five passions of the mind. The first is lust. It's not bad that we desire love or food or drink or anything else. It's when the desire becomes too much, when it's too much of a good thing.

We're the path of moderation.

We're the path of moderation. For example, I discourage alcoholic beverages. I'm not going to say, "Absolutely none," but I think anyone who is sincerely interested in moving along the spiritual path in the most direct way won't drink because alcoholic beverages cloud the mind and dull the awareness. To me it's a contradiction when people say they are interested in unfolding spiritually and at the same time they can't get along without their drink. On the other hand, some medicines use alcohol as a preservative. You take those because it's part of the healing process.

An appetite for food, for love, and for drink are

all OK because they're part of living here. It's when the desire becomes too great that it's too much of a good thing.

The second passion is anger. Sometimes you feel you have been wronged and you need to stand up for yourself. And you make a point of it—you do whatever you can to correct the situation, and then you move on. But some people object too much. Too much of a good thing in this case becomes anger and its children, like criticism and gossip. These are all signs of anger.

The third passion is greed. We want things. We should have things because we need things to live here. For instance, don't try to get through a Minnesota winter without a coat. You need a coat. You probably don't need twenty coats; maybe that's when you're crossing the line.

We all occasionally take too much of something. It can be chocolate cake. It can be anything.

Another passion of the mind, the fourth, is attachment. It means when we have home, family, or one of twenty coats—whatever—and we like them too much. We do not like to let go of them. Again, it's just too much of a good thing.

The fifth passion of the mind is vanity. There's nothing wrong with having a good opinion of yourself. In fact, as a spiritual creation of God, wouldn't you have a good opinion of yourself? Sure you would. But vanity is too much of a good thing. It's when you begin thinking you are better than the other creations of God around you. You think you are a lot better, and you lord it over others. This is vanity.

Any of these passions—lust, anger, greed, attachment, and vanity—are simply just too much of a good thing.

When the desire becomes too great then it's too much of a good thing.

FIVE VIRTUES

There are also five virtues—ways to offset the passions. One is discrimination. Discrimination just means making the right choices. Some people have an uncanny knack for making the wrong choices, and that's why they have the problems they do. They'll get into one unhappy marriage after another after another. Two, three, four times the mate turns out to be an alcoholic. You say, "What bad luck!" But it's not bad luck. Soul, who is making the choice, has poor discrimination and makes poor choices.

How do you change this? First you have to look at your own weaknesses. Then you have to also know how to grow and develop spiritually. Generally it's through singing the ancient name of God, HU. This or one of the other spiritual exercises helps.

The second of the five virtues is a little bit hard to put into one word, so I'll use two: *forgiveness* or *tolerance*. They are similar. If someone has wronged you, you try to straighten it out. And when it's straightened out, you let it go. Tolerance means if someone doesn't believe the way you do—in politics, religion, whatever—you let them have their own space. You let them have their own mind.

Contentment is the third of the five virtues that offset the five passions. The apostle Paul in the New Testament said, "I have learned, in whatsoever state I am, therewith to be content." You find contentment very much out of sorts in a socialist state—and I include the United States and Germany, because they are strongly socialistic. Because people are never happy with what they have. They always want what belongs to someone else.

This is the whole premise of a socialist state. Distribution of the wealth means that if someone has

> There are also five virtues— ways to offset the passions.

earned more because they have worked more, it counts for nothing. You distribute the wealth anyway. And people are never content. Because if they get something for nothing, they want more and more and more. In our own country we find that this is actually one of the weaknesses of the democratic system, as the ancient Greeks found. Once people are empowered, they realize that they can steal the property of others through laws; and there's no stopping them. They use courts and laws. People seek judgments and take other people's property through the court system.

There's no respect for property rights. It slowly winds downhill. Somewhere it has to turn around. I'm talking about the spiritual nature of things: in the spiritual scheme of things, under spiritual law, you have to earn your way in life. You don't get a free lunch simply because you ask for it.

You might be able to get by with this for one lifetime, and some people do. But it's the big lie of socialism to believe that you can get something for nothing, and if you can get it through the law, better yet.

Sometimes there is so little justice in the law. Especially as a democracy grows in strength and as the laws become more crippling. A society with more laws generally means that the society is slipping in spirituality.

Next comes the virtue of detachment. No matter what you have, don't like it too much, because the nature of this lower world is that everything passes. Children grow up. The house gets old; the building wears down. We don't have the strength to take care of it the way we did when we were young. As people get closer to retirement they have to let go. Some people find it very hard, especially when the closets

No matter what you have, don't like it too much, because the nature of this lower world is that everything passes.

are full, the attic is full, the basement is full, and you can barely get one car in the two-car garage. It's too full. So this virtue is detachment.

If you want to overcome vanity, become humble.

Another is humility. If you want to overcome vanity, become humble. This is one of those things you can't just tell somebody. You can't say, "Here, I shall touch you with this microphone, and you will have humility." Unless there's a short in the cord.

AT THE POST OFFICE

My wife was at the post office one day, using the photocopier. She had papers she needed to copy before she could mail them, and the papers were spread out over the copier.

Just about that time a young boy walks up. His mother was in another part of the post office, mailing letters or packages. My wife has her quarters laid out on the copier, and the little boy wants to help. "Well, you can put a quarter in for me," she says. He wants to put them all in. She says, "No, I don't think I'm going to need them all." So he's thinking about this. Maybe she won't need them all. His mother is calling to him: Don't bother the lady. So he leaves, but he comes back a few minutes later, and he starts chatting, asking questions. And he says, "Can I have a quarter?" My wife says, "Ask your mother. She'll give you one."

This kid knows. He's thinking, *Fat chance of that. Right. My mother's going to give me a quarter just because I ask.* So he starts playing with the paper clips laid out next to the copier. He wants to put them into the coin slot. My wife says, "If you do that people won't be able to use the copier." The mother calls again from the other side of the room, and the little boy runs off. When he comes back a little bit later, my wife sees that he's got a little Spider-Man toy. "What's his name?" my wife asks. He says, "I don't talk to strangers."

My wife says, "I don't either. Then I guess we better not talk to each other."

They stand there very quietly; he's making a daisy chain with the paper clips, and she's finishing the copying. Then the mother calls the little boy over, and they go outside.

I'm standing outside waiting for my wife. As the mother and child come out the door, the kid runs down the stairs. The mother says, "Jeffrey, don't run down the stairs." I'm thinking, *This kid has probably heard, "Jeffrey, don't do this. Jeffrey, don't do that. Jeffrey stop now. One more time, Jeffrey, you're grounded." He's heard it his whole life. He doesn't mind anymore. His eyes glaze over, his ears are filled with wax.*

It had snowed; the ground was slippery and wet. The post office had put up concrete blocks right at the edge of the sidewalk so that vehicles couldn't drive up on the sidewalk and block it. Jeffrey begins trying to balance on them like he is walking on a railroad track, but they're very slippery and wet. Mother says, "Jeffrey, get off there; they were not meant for walking on."

So Jeffrey gets off, but Jeffrey doesn't really care because Jeffrey's going to be up to some other mischief. He's not a bad boy, but he is active and curious. He has to try everything. And his mother's job is to let him know the rules of society—where the walls are. "There's a wall, Jeffrey. Don't go over that wall." Apples are on the other side, but Mother says, "Don't go over that wall; they're not yours," teaching him about the rights and property of others.

She was doing her job. And Jeffrey was doing his job. He is supposed to learn and explore — do everything he can to know more about this world before he leaves. Her job is to teach him where to go or not to go, how his rights stop where the rights of others begin. It was a very good education.

I found this conflict interesting.

When I start talking about the five passions, it's like saying "No, no, no, no, no." Pretty soon people get tired. *I've heard that before. We'll wait until he finishes, and then when he's done maybe it's time for lunch,* they say to themselves.

LEARN TODAY'S LESSONS

I put together five points to help you master your spiritual destiny — just five points that may help.

Point number one: Forget the past, and learn the spiritual lessons of today.

A woman we'll call Shirley is a very upbeat person and a wonderful administrator. She works in a university as an educator. In the past she had been a dean. Lately the family savings had begun to run down, so she found a job as an associate dean. It means being number two, whereas before she had been number one. She found very quickly after she was hired that the dean was a very capable and compassionate woman, but there was one thing she could not do. That was to tell people who were not doing their jobs to do their jobs. The dean did not have this capability. But this was just one of the natural skills that Shirley had learned through her work.

The university was a very successful one, but they had a lot of personnel problems — people couldn't get along. So Shirley started using a certain approach: she would try to help people to work as a

Point number one: Forget the past, and learn the spiritual lessons of today.

team. And she succeeded. She got one department after another straightened out. She would ask basic questions: What did they do? Who did they do it for? Was it still worth doing? And if they could do anything else, what would it be? Pretty soon she got people talking about the strengths and the weaknesses of the place they worked.

One of the departments was in trouble. It was the department that used television and other methods to work with students off campus. The manager was newly hired. He had heard of the success Shirley had had with other departments, so he called her.

He said he was just about ready to lose his job. The people in his department did absolutely what they pleased, and he couldn't bring order to the place. Was there something she could do?

Shirley looked the whole thing over. She had only been at the university a few months, and she didn't know all the ways things were done there; but she saw this was a critical situation. She had to help. And if she was going to do anything, it had to be done right away. So she called a meeting of the staff. They came together, and she found that the people were very angry. So she asked the four questions again: What did they do? Who did they do it for? Was it still worth doing? And if they could do anything else, what would it be?

As the group responded to these four questions, things began to change, but the anger was still there. The staff could not accept the person who was their new manager.

Then the Mahanta, the Inner Master, gave her an inspiration. A fifth question came to her very unexpectedly. The question was What is it that you did in the past you no longer do now? So she opened up the

Then the Mahanta, the Inner Master, gave her an inspiration. A fifth question came to her very unexpectedly.

The first point to mastering your spiritual destiny is to forget the past, let it go, and learn the spiritual lessons today.

past. Remember our topic here—the first point to mastering your spiritual destiny is to forget the past, let it go, and learn the spiritual lessons today.

It turned out that during the 1980s this department was funded by grants from oil companies. A lot of money came in. They had the best equipment, and the rapport between people was good. They all felt good about what they did. But in the nineties, the recession hit, and grants from oil companies were cut back. Suddenly the university was in trouble. They began cutting back, and this department was one of the first to feel the pinch.

Soon much of their staff was laid off, their equipment began to get old, and they were no longer able to provide good programming for the students off campus. Morale went straight downhill.

The new manager walked into this. He didn't realize the history of this department: how it used to be successful; how it used to mean something to work there; how working there had been a privilege and a joy. Today it wasn't a joy anymore.

After Shirley asked these five questions and heard their responses, she said to them, "Describe to me how you feel working here." They used phrases such as "slow death," "picking the carcass clean," and other very negative images. Can you imagine that these people had been working in this area all this time?

Shirley wrote these things on the board. She said, "This is how you feel now." And she put three boxes up on the board.

"The first box is the old construct, the past, how things were. The second is the present construct. And the third is the new construct, the future," she told them.

These people were all locked in the past. They

were locked in one of the five stages of mourning. Usually there's anger, grief, sadness, and then rebuilding and hope. These people were stuck in the past, way back when the department got cut back, back at the stage of anger, stage one of this whole process of letting go of the past.

Mourning is letting the past go. If you want to move forward in your own life but you've got a lot of problems, it's probably because you're hanging on to something in the past. You're trying to solve today's problems with yesterday's solutions. They didn't work then, they're not going to work now. As people get older and older, they find it harder to come up with new solutions.

Shirley was trying to break through this. So they asked her what they could do. She told them, "Bury the dead. Forget the past. Bury all these dead images, these negative images. Bury them. Let the past go." She explained the five stages of mourning. "How do we go about it?" they asked.

Shirley said, "It's like this. The train's ready to leave the station. If you're going to be on the train, you'll all have to be going the same direction. If you can't change the present so you can have a happier future, you'll never be happy here. If that's the case, you owe it to yourself to go someplace else and get another job."

It set them back on their heels, and they had to think this over. But she found that even the very hard cases in the department began to turn around, and things looked better for a moment.

Whenever a change comes, this can happen. Human nature being what it is, one person may have a revelation and enlightenment and turn around; others won't.

Human nature being what it is, one person may have a revelation and enlightenment and turn around; others won't.

Shirley had said to them that if they couldn't change the present by letting go of the past, they were never going to be able to make a better future for themselves. They owed it to themselves to either change or go find some other place to work. Because by going to another place they would have changed their outer circumstances anyway, even though they hadn't made a change inside.

Reader's Digest had a good quote about this: "It's OK to glance at the past, just don't stare."

Look for a new way to solve a stubborn problem.

LOOK FOR A NEW WAY

Here's the second point about how you can learn to master your spiritual destiny: Look for a new way to solve a stubborn problem. It sounds like the same thing, but it's a little different. It's adding another dimension.

A woman in Eckankar was very concerned about her father. He was being treated at the Veterans Administration hospital in the city and was taking new medication. This new medicine was making his pulse go from eighty beats per minute to 155. His next appointment wasn't for three weeks, but the woman was trying to convince her father to go earlier and get that prescription changed. She knew the current prescription was going to harm him.

But he was a stubborn old guy. "My appointment's in three weeks," he said. "This is what the doctor gave me, so this is OK."

The father was determined to wait the three weeks. But the daughter thought, *He's not going to make it.* So one evening, after a very exhausting day at work, she came home, plopped herself into a chair, picked up the phone, and called her dad to learn how his pulse was doing. It was still near 155. She didn't know what to do. She knew it was something that needed attention, but she was discouraged as she hung up after the phone call.

Suddenly— out of thin air— a voice said, "Hello, anybody home?"

The woman looked around, but nobody was there. *It's been a hard day,* she thought. *I've been worrying about my dad; maybe I'm losing my mind.*

The voice scared her a bit, so she went into the kitchen and sat down. The cats were there, and they all came around her, hoping for dinner. Then the voice came again, "Lights are on, but nobody's home."

Now she became angry. "If you're so smart, you'll come up with the solution," she said out loud to the voice, and the cats ran. They'd never heard her talk like this, because she was usually a very composed person. The cats scattered to all parts of the house.

And the voice said, "Simple. Have the doctor call him."

The voice said, "Simple. Have the doctor call him."

Her brows furrow, come down low on the forehead, and it feels a little bit like the Neanderthal incarnation. "Oh, yeah, right!" she said.

The next morning the woman called the VA hospital, but she couldn't remember the doctor's name. The receptionist put her through to the first doctor she could find. The doctor came on the line, "Hello, this is Dr. Moran." *That's it,* the woman thought, amazed. *That's the name.* This was her father's doctor. "Dr. Moran," she said, "here's the problem." And they went through the whole thing.

"Of course, I'd be happy to call," Dr. Moran said. "We have to change the medication." Everything worked out very nicely.

So point number two: Look for a new way to solve a stubborn problem. In the past she had tried to reason with a stubborn father. It didn't work. And what was she trying this time? She was trying to reason with a stubborn father. Would the father listen? No. Why? Because he was stubborn. It was an old problem that wouldn't go away. So this voice came to her and it said, "Have the doctor call him." It was the flip side of the coin.

DO YOUR VERY BEST

Point number three to help you master your spiritual destiny: Whatever you undertake, do it to the best of your ability. If necessary, do it even better.

A very good carpenter, Jim, was kind enough to build the benches in the Temple of ECK vestibule. Visitors can sit down when they come in, if they want to talk and visit. He built the benches very carefully.

Whatever you undertake, do it to the best of your ability. If necessary, do it even better.

Over the years a few of the benches began to split along the top. The design of the benches is called a breadboard design: the grain of the boards runs lengthwise, and then at the end there are two pieces of wood that run across. As Jim researched, he found that this is a common problem with this design. It looks very good, but any great changes in humidity or temperature, and the benches tend to split right down the center.

Finally Jim found an article in a magazine that showed how to build this breadboard design with a floating joint to accommodate the expansion and shrinkage. And so he fixed the benches and built this joint in.

This is point number three: Whatever you undertake, do it to the best of your ability. Jim made excellent benches. But the temperature and humidity, which can be very extreme in Minnesota, caused him to have to do it over again. He could have just let it go.

But he didn't. There's a saying that a good carpenter always covers his mistakes. But that's an average craftsman. A really good one makes it right. So if it's necessary to do something over, then do it even better. And that's what Jim did; he put in floating joints.

LEADER OR OUTCAST?

Point number four to help you master your spiritual destiny: Being different can make you an outcast or a leader. Sometime you need to make a choice. In other words, sometime you're going to have to decide whether you're going to be an outcast or a leader.

One of the staff at the ECK Temple, Carol, went to Cocoa Beach, Florida, for an ECK seminar. She met with the ECK youth, and she found that their biggest concern was not fitting in. They were ECKists in a Christian community. We in Eckankar have our own beliefs the way Hindus and the Buddhists do. Millions of people have beliefs different from those of Christianity, which is hard for some people in a Christian society to believe. But people are born, they live, and they die. And they come back too, which some Christians can't believe, but which other religions do. We have our differences.

These youth were in an awful position. If they mentioned that they're ECKists, right away their friends would say, "You're going to hell."

There's a saying I read in the Patrick O'Brian Commodore series of seventeen novels about the sea. These novels are a very good study on friendship, character, and everything else. But he said sailors sometimes would catch an albatross and put a blob of red paint on it. The albatross would fly off, and the other albatrosses would kill it because it was different. If there's a chicken in the henhouse that's

Being different can make you an outcast or a leader. Sometime you need to make a choice.

not well, the other chickens will go after it. It's this way in society too: if you're different, you're the albatross with a red splotch of paint on you.

And the other people, the other albatrosses, have the purest white coats; they can feel very smug and self-righteous about themselves because they go to church on Sunday. But it's this lack of tolerance which is one of the spiritual blemishes that Soul will have to address sometime—either in this lifetime or in some future lifetime. Soul is going to have to learn to overcome intolerance.

The way life works is that usually you have to have the experience of being in the minority in some way.

The way life works is that usually you have to have the experience of being in the minority in some way. Either you have to be in the wheelchair, white in a black society, black in a white society, rich when everybody else says poverty is the rule, or the poor person in a rich household. Somewhere along the line you're going to have to learn tolerance.

One of these young people was in her early twenties. "You think you have problems," she told the other youth. This girl had red hair, and all through grade school she got teased about her red hair. And when she got in ECK, she had red hair and she was in Eckankar. So she got it doubly.

One time when she was eight, she had a personal inner experience where she learned that the path of ECK was for her. So suddenly she had this change in attitude. She said, "I have red hair; it's beautiful. I'm going to be proud of it. And I'm in ECK. It is the teaching which is my teaching, the very highest I could find for myself in this lifetime. It is my path." And she stood her ground on this. She found that when she had confidence in her red hair and her spiritual path, other people gave her respect.

So again, point number four: Being different can

make you an outcast or a leader. Sometime you need
to make a choice.

TELL OTHERS ABOUT ECK

Point number five to help you master your spiritual destiny: Tell others about the teachings of ECK.

This ties in with the greater spiritual purpose,
why Soul has come here: to become a Co-worker with
God. That is the main mission each Soul is trying to
accomplish. But it's a big bite. And so we work on
smaller bites.

A woman in Los Angeles, California, applied to
the Department of Motor Vehicles for a vanity license
plate. It was a personalized license plate. It was
H U 4 L O V E. She was very proud of this license
plate. One New Year's Eve as she was driving home,
a car full of people pulled up alongside her at a
stoplight. A man yelled something out of the window
that she couldn't hear. *Well, it's L.A.,* she thought to
herself. *You never know here, but they look OK.* So
she rolled her window down.

"Is your name HU?" the man yelled across at her.

"No," she said. The man turned, looked at his wife
and the other couple in the car, then turned back to
the woman. "I just lost a hundred dollars," he said.

The light changed, and they went driving off to
the next traffic light. Both cars stopped, and the man
leaned on his horn again, waving his arms. She rolled
down her window, and he said, "You sure your name's
not HU?" She said, "No," and as the light was about
to change the wife leaned over her husband and
asked, "What does HU mean?" With just five seconds
to go, the woman said, "HU is a name for God." The
light changed, and they all drove off.

*Point number
five to help
you master
your spiritual
destiny: Tell
others about
the teachings
of ECK.*

She said the experience really made her New Year's Eve.

Light and Sound of God

This is the purpose of Soul—to be here and let other people know about the Light and Sound of God. Most people know about the Light nowadays because of media coverage on near-death experiences. But very few people know about the Sound. These are the two aspects of God. This is the Voice of God, or the Holy Spirit. The Holy Spirit, the Light and Sound of God, and the Voice of God are all the same thing.

In short, the Light and Sound of God equals the love of God. This is why it's so important.

Soul exists because God loves It. In other words, you exist because God loves you. That's why the Light and Sound of God, the Voice of God, is so important. It is the Holy Spirit.

Soul exists because God loves It. In other words, you exist because God loves you.

Soul's Journey

I would like to mention a book that is going to be very helpful to some of you. It sounds similar to the title of one of my own books. It's by someone else. As far as I know he has no connection at all with the path of ECK. My book is called *Journey of Soul*, and this one is *Journey of Souls* by Dr. Michael Newton. He's a state-certified master hypnotherapist from California.

People worry about hypnotism. But again, we are a path of moderation. We do what's necessary. This doctor works with people to help them overcome problems that they can't handle themselves.

The book is a study that he has done recording what patients have learned through hypnosis about their lives—and not just past lives. He touches on that briefly, but that's not the focus of his study. It's a very, very good study of what Souls do between lives. How they evaluate the life they have just finished. How happy they are with their progress, how unhappy.

I have to mention one thing about it: He talks about guides and teachers. These guides and teachers belong to the structure of the Lords of Karma. They're part of that hierarchy. He doesn't know that, he doesn't call them that. But they are part of the structure, the hierarchy, of the Lords of Karma.

The book tells why people incarnate in certain places at certain times. Why did they come here? Why do people have certain health conditions? Why do people get born into certain countries, certain families? Why do they do it? In a socialist state the feeling is always that someone in government knows better. Someone with a clever mind can fix all the problems of the society.

The fact is no Soul comes to this earth born equal.

The fact is no Soul comes to this earth born equal. And no government intervention will ever make it so. Not to say that people shouldn't try to improve conditions, but you have to improve conditions by not breaking other spiritual laws. If you want to give to a charity, you don't rob the poor box to do it. In socialism, the end justifies the means. It's the lie of socialism. Because it's based on the wrong spiritual premise.

This book also takes a look at the structure of karma. Why people suffer as they do in this lifetime. Not because something was dumped on them. It's something they agreed to do in this lifetime because they needed to polish some spiritual aspect of their divine nature.

Divine nature here is immature, unpolished. Soul is eternal, but immature. It hasn't got the experience.

Divine nature here is immature, unpolished. Soul is eternal, but immature. It hasn't got the experience. And this is why the path of ECK is based so strongly on experience.

I realize you cannot tell people to do something when they haven't understood the reason for doing it. Usually the best way we understand things is by pain, and that's why there is pain in this world. And lots of people don't want to come back. You'll find some very interesting aspects in this book about how many bodies a Soul can run at the same time. It's very interesting.

The author has written a very good book. He's going to open your eyes in many ways, but he also has some limitations. For instance, the higher he goes in the worlds he explores through the people he has hypnotized, the darker the light becomes. In other words, he says the energy around immature Souls is white. As they get a little more experience, yellow. Then it goes into the deeper colors like blue, light blue, dark blue, and violet. He thinks violet is the most advanced stage. He doesn't know.

The reason the colors seem to get darker in the lower worlds, according to his study of energy, is that there is a dividing line between the lower worlds which includes the Physical world; the Astral, or emotional, world; and then the Mental worlds—the Causal, Mental, and Etheric Planes. That's the farthest he can go.

These are the lower worlds. But there is a dividing line, a black void, between the spiritual-material worlds down here and the pure spiritual worlds above. In the pure spiritual worlds, the Soul Plane, the light is a yellowish white. As one goes higher, the light is whiter and whiter, more brilliant, until it goes right into the heart of God—which is the purest, most absolute white.

In other words, he cannot get through this area we call Yreka, a tunnel between the Etheric Plane and the Soul Plane. It's a black zone. Souls that are ready, go across this dark area with the Mahanta—they can't cross it unless they are with the Mahanta. That's why the position of the Mahanta, the Living ECK Master is called the Light Giver, the Wayshower. He gets Soul through this dark area.

There is a dark area between each plane, between the Physical and the Astral Planes, for example. Then there's another dark zone between the Astral and the Causal. And so on up. But there's a great dividing line between the spiritual-material worlds—the lower worlds—and the pure spiritual worlds above. And this is that dark zone, the black tunnel. It's just pitch black. No Soul can go through it without the help of the Mahanta.

I think you'll find the book interesting. I mentioned the limitations of the colors and why they occur because he doesn't understand everything. He doesn't claim to. He's a very good researcher. It's a good book about the destiny of Souls, and that's why I mention it in this talk on mastering your spiritual destiny.

Realize that, whether you are Christian or ECKist or Hindu or Buddhist, you do have a spiritual destiny. You came here for a spiritual purpose. And the teachings of ECK can help you find what that purpose is.

Realize that, whether you are Christian or ECKist or Hindu or Buddhist, you do have a spiritual destiny. You came here for a spiritual purpose.

Temple of ECK Worship Service, Chanhassen, Minnesota, Sunday, March 3, 1996

Divine Spirit was saying thank you to her—for doing something just simply for love.

5

Just for Love

I've been spending the last two years trying to regain my health and have made slow steps in that regard. One of the doctors I go to is a Chinese acupuncturist. He was raised at a Christian mission in mainland China, so he speaks English very well. He came to the United States about twelve years ago.

He's one of those people in the health professions who is very interested in healing. In China he had spent twenty-five or thirty years in a field of surgery. But rather than go through all kinds of requalifications here, he took up acupuncture. That's how he's been taking care of himself and other people for the last twelve years. He's a very good man.

When I first came to him, I was very ill, but gradually my strength has improved. I've been going to him for a year and a half or more, and each session takes two hours. He puts acupuncture needles in my back first—to support different organs. Then after twenty minutes he takes them out and puts needles down the front of me.

There was a time when I said I'd never go to an acupuncturist, but you learn. And I keep going back because it helps.

KEEP YOUR SPIRITS UP

Over the months he gradually pieced together that I was connected with Eckankar. He was always fascinated with my wife. She's an editor and does many other things at the Eckankar Spiritual Center. Whenever we come, she sits in the room with me during the first twenty-minute session. Then after the doctor puts needles in for the rest of the session, she goes into another room where he has a little table. The first day, she asked him, "Is it all right if I do some work here?" He said it was fine, so she pulled out all these manuscripts and set to work.

One day he said to me, "Your wife, she is an editor, yes?" I said, "Yes, she's an editor and a very good one." He didn't say much, but it looked like he was putting all this together. One day he said, "Your wife, she is your nurse, she is your cook, she is your driver, and she is your editor." He seemed very impressed by that.

She doesn't just work to meet a schedule, to get something done. She works because she loves to.

My wife does have an amazing capacity for work and love. She doesn't just work to meet a schedule, to get something done. She works because she loves to. And she loves me too.

One day, he seemed to have figured everything out. He knew that I was the spiritual leader of Eckankar. I said, "This ought to be really good storytelling when you go home and tell your family, 'Today I stuck a spiritual leader full of needles.'" He thought that was pretty funny; he has a quiet sense of humor.

One week when I went to see him, he put a needle between my big toe and second toe on each foot, and they hurt a lot. So I asked him, "What are those for?"

"Those are for your spirits," he said.

"Oh, OK," I said. For a couple of weeks afterward,

he didn't use needles in those spots, but he watched to see if I was paying attention as he put needles in other places. Then one day he told me, "Take your socks off," and he stuck a needle between my first two toes again. He said, "Do you remember what that is for?"

I said, "It's for my spirits." And he says, "That's right. You're the spiritual leader, and we have to keep your spirits up."

I do know that when my spirits get low and the needle sticks them down there, they go the other direction.

BRINGING BALANCE

One day he said, out of the blue, "The Buddhists try to take people out of this world, and the Christians try to get people to live in this world. What does Eckankar try to do?"

You know, you're lying on the table waiting for needles, not exactly in a missionary mode. I said, "Both." He just stopped, looked at me, nodded his head, and went on with his work as if that was very natural and a normal thing to say. And then I just said a few words by way of explanation: "There are some people whose heads are in the clouds, and they don't know how to make it down here. They need balance, they need help in learning how to live here and make things work. There are other people who are out of balance in the other direction. They're so caught up in the material things of life that they have forgotten their dreams. I try to help these people too. I try to bring a balance of heaven and earth together so that these people can find love in their lives."

I try to bring a balance of heaven and earth together so that these people can find love in their lives.

He seemed very satisfied with that, and he hasn't said anything more now for a couple of weeks. But he usually springs these kinds of questions on me. He works very quietly. Then all of a sudden he'll ask his questions.

Just for love. This is the whole purpose of life.

JUST FOR LOVE

Just for love. This is the whole purpose of life.

People pursue truth. They'll go to the far corners of the world. They'll go through one religion after another, they'll become atheists, maybe agnostics, and run through all the different philosophies and religious teachings. But until they find love, they've not found truth.

And if they didn't find love, they will never find freedom, spiritual freedom. So they are driven to search the world over to try to find true love.

One day an ECKist in Switzerland was driving down the road. She saw a little girl by the side of the road trying to cross. To give her plenty of time to cross safely, the woman stopped her car, and the little girl crossed the road. The woman began driving again. After she'd gone just a short distance, a policeman waved at her.

Right away, she felt for her seat belt. She didn't have it on. It's a law in Switzerland as it is in many states in the United States that you have to wear a seat belt. She was worried. She thought, *Oh, he's going to pull me over and give me a ticket because I've broken the law.* She was very concerned.

But then, as she drove closer, she saw that the policeman was smiling. He had waved to her to thank her for having stopped for the child. So she drove on, much relieved.

She thought, *How often do we have one of the five passions or one of its children, like guilt, hanging over us! So that when the love of God comes down to say "Thank you" or "I love you" or something like this through one of the other human beings on earth, we're so closed up with fear that we miss the blessing.*

She realized she had let the child cross in front of her car just for love. Divine Spirit was saying thank you to her—for doing something just simply for love. But because she felt guilty for not wearing a seat belt and thinking she had broken a law, she was afraid. And this shut her spiritual eyes and ears. She couldn't hear, and she couldn't see.

FEAR OF LIVING

Perhaps the greatest lesson that Soul has to learn when It comes to earth is how to overcome fear. It can be fear of any kind: fear of public speaking, for instance. Public speaking is one of the more fearful things that many people have to do. There are many other fears: Are you going to succeed at work? Are you going to be able to hold on to your job? Is there going to be enough money to pay the bills next month? Is your health OK? One fear after another. We become too afraid, too much a victim of fear—and that's the only valid time you can call yourself a victim. When we become a victim of fear, we shut out the beautiful, divine part of life.

This fear is, after all, a fear of living. And this is what Eckankar is here to help you overcome, this fear of living.

I've noticed that young people drive faster than older people. I don't know if the difference is more fear in older people. But I know when I was young, I drove a lot faster than I would now. Because if you haven't bumped yourself enough, you probably haven't learned to be careful. Children walk fast when they're first learning to walk. They run into

Perhaps the greatest lesson that Soul has to learn when It comes to earth is how to overcome fear.

something, they trip, they stub their toes, they do all these things. And somewhere along the line, they learn that it hurts to stub your toe. They learn that if you go a little bit slower and walk a little more carefully, you're not going to stub your toe. Life becomes that much easier, and you can go on to other challenges, bigger places to stub bigger toes.

A LITTLE HOT SAUCE

I write monthly discourses for those who are studying the ECK teachings and are members of Eckankar. In this discourse, or letter, I try to pass along some spiritual insight as best I can.

But it's still up to people to put their creative faculties to work and get something out of each discourse. Some people do, and some people don't.

A young mother who is an ECKist got one of these monthly discourses in the mail one day. In this particular discourse I asked people to do something purely for love without expecting anyone to say, "Thanks a lot for what you did; I appreciate it."

This woman has a family, and she spends a lot of time cooking and cleaning, doing laundry, taking the children to the store, and all sorts of other things. She knew this was all for love. But she wondered if there wasn't something else that she could do that would be just for love—something outside her ordinary, everyday routine.

She was thinking about it one night as she was making her husband's lunch for the next day. She looked in the refrigerator. All she had was two-day-old hamburger and bread. *Well, the hamburger's probably OK, but how am I going to make it taste good? Is he going to eat this?* she wondered.

She decided she would put a lot of love into that

It's up to people to put their creative faculties to work and get something out of each discourse.

two-day-old hamburger, because it needed it. Then she got a nudge from her inner side that said, "Yeah, love, and try some of that hot sauce too." After a couple of nudges she finally put on the hot sauce.

The next day when her husband came home, he said, "That was a great sandwich! What did you have in there?" *Thank goodness I listened to the little nudge that said, "Put on the hot sauce,"* the woman thought, *because the love's already there.* These are small things that people do, just for love, expecting no thanks, no one to notice, no one to say, "Well, that was a good thing you just did."

A MEASURE OF LOVE

In winter, this woman also likes to put out old bread and cereal for the birds and squirrels. The birds come from all around. But one particular day as she put out the bread, all that came were a squirrel and a crow.

She remembered that when she first started putting out food for the birds and the animals, she used to shoo away the crow and any other not-so-pretty birds. She thought that if she was going to put out food, it ought to be for the "pretty" birds.

But when she got this assignment in a monthly discourse—to do something just for love—she decided she would put out the food for any bird or animal that came. Of course, first in line are the squirrels and crows and sparrows.

It took a while, but soon she could accept all birds and all animals coming out to the feeding station in her yard. And with that change, love began to fill her heart.

With that change, love began to fill her heart.

When someone is getting more love in their heart, how do you measure that? Do you get out a little scale and say, "We're going to measure and see if indeed you have two ounces more of love this year than you had last year." How do you quantify love? Love is not one of those things you can sell; it's not one of those things you can take to the market and have people admire. It's not something you can put up in an art gallery where people say, "Oh, love! Look at that, that's a good example right there on the wall."

No, love is just a very quiet, personal little thing. It brings fulfillment, but more importantly, it brings spiritual freedom. Because love is truth.

WHAT'S YOUR PURPOSE HERE?

Often I see people who say they are trying to ferret out untruth. It's an interesting situation. They take the negative side: They don't look for truth, they don't promote truth, they try to ferret out untruth. It's a profession for a lot of people. All Souls have a reason for coming here, and they agree to that reason before they come. Then they either do it well or they don't do it well. And some people's whole purpose is to ferret out untruth.

Other people's whole purpose in being here is to promote truth, love, and life. It's not right or wrong in either case. It's just simply what people have agreed to do before they came into this life.

And as such, we find that there is no one who is a victim. Major turning points in a person's life have all been agreed to beforehand.

People do have free will to get off the beaten path, to not follow the path that they have agreed to go along for certain spiritual lessons in this lifetime. But when they do this, it usually means they're not moving straight ahead in their spiritual life. Between lives, they have to come to an accounting with

Major turning points in a person's life have all been agreed to beforehand.

themselves. They have to look at their life and say, "OK, what did I set out to accomplish in that last life? It was so and so. Now, did I accomplish that? Did I make great strides in the right direction, or did I get off track? Did my attention wander from my spiritual goal?" People are their own worst critics between lives when it comes to seeing what they accomplished and what they failed to accomplish.

That's why the idea of a victim—especially in the sense that is so prevalent today—is a spiritual fallacy. People say, "I got fired. It's so unjust. I'm a victim." Often it's an opportunity for people to grow because they had come to a dead end in that position.

People say, "I got fired. It's so unjust. I'm a victim." Often it's an opportunity for people to grow because they had come to a dead end in that position.

LOVE IS ITS OWN REWARD

A woman was talking to her parents and her brother about family matters. One of the things that came up was that the child of her brother—her nephew—was addicted to sugar. So her mother said, "I would very much like to spoil him, but I just can't bring myself to give him any kind of sugar snacks because he gets too many already." She felt like a frustrated grandma who can't spoil her grandchild.

"Don't worry about it," the daughter said. "You've got two grand-pups here at my place. You can spoil them." She calls the two dogs Charlie and Jess.

Charlie and Jess like to go for walks, so whenever Grams comes over, they figure it's because she has come to spoil them by going for a walk. And then they go on very long walks with her.

One day Grams came over to help her daughter do some work in the house, and they worked for three or four hours. When they finished, Grams went upstairs to the bathroom to clean up before she went home. As she came out of the bathroom, she saw the two little pups were sitting outside the bathroom door looking at her with great big eyes. "Would you please take us for a walk?" they seemed to be saying. "That is why you came! You can't just go home and not take us for a walk."

Grams looked at the little dogs and said to her daughter, "They certainly have a way of projecting their message, don't they?" So before she left, she took them for a walk as their little treat. She did this just simply for love. She didn't expect any thanks. You know how it is: Love is its own reward.

She didn't expect any thanks. You know how it is: Love is its own reward.

CHOOSING TO GIVE

Sometimes when you go out looking for love, you find that this formula of doing something for love doesn't work. It doesn't pay back in fulfillment. A man who lives in the greater New York City area had made a rule never to stop and pick up any motorist in trouble—a good rule because there are danger zones in any metropolitan area. Thieves have figured out all kinds of ways to trap someone and rob them and do whatever else they want.

It was 3:00 a.m., and he and his wife were driving home from a party. Along an isolated parkway they saw a stranded car and three women standing outside by the headlights, waving their arms for him to stop.

Normally the man would never have stopped, especially with his wife in the car, but this time he did. It turned out the three women actually did have a flat tire. So he quickly changed the tire, and as he was getting back into his own car, one of the women said, "Please take some money. We prayed to God to come help us; we've been out here two hours and nobody came."

"I can't take any money," the man said. He just felt grateful that he had done the charitable thing and gotten away with it. But in the following days, as he thought about the incident, he was still concerned that he had stopped. *I simply did it for love,* he told himself, *even though I may not have been using my best judgment at the time.*

A little while later he was driving on another parkway, and he saw another car pulled over, the hood up, and a man standing alongside, waving his hand as if he needed help. Inside the car was a woman and a child. The man knew that this was often a favorite setup for robbers.

There are so many immature Souls in the world because of the overpopulation problem. Not that there aren't enough mature Souls to come to all the little bodies that are available—there are. But it's a very sad thing today. It's one of those times, a darker age of humanity, where people are not as aware of their divine self nor of the divine self of others.

The ECKist looked at the man and wondered, Is he telling the truth?

The ECKist pulled over. The man in the car told him, "I was in a restaurant, and I lost my wallet"— the old story. The ECKist looked at the man and wondered, *Is he telling the truth?* He decided no, but he said, "Listen, whether you lost your wallet or not, here's some money to get you some gas even though you know this is a very involved way of begging."

"No, no," the man said, "give me your name and address, because as soon as I get home I'm going to send you a check for twenty dollars to pay back the money you've given me." The ECKist was very generous to give twenty dollars. I don't know how much I would have given if I had been there.

And then the ECKist drove off, and the man and his wife and little child drove off too. The ECKist said later, "The man must never have gotten home because I never got a check. I wasn't expecting one; I did it just for love."

FREE CHEESE

The immature Souls in this world are always taking, taking, taking. They'll use any excuse: "I'm a victim," for instance. Then they get attorneys—who often are immature Souls too. So you've got this whole group of people who are always taking, because they think they can without having to pay for whatever they receive. It's one of the old lies of this world that so many people fall for: something for nothing.

It's one of the old lies of this world that so many people fall for: something for nothing.

Someone sent me a poster of a mouse standing by a mousetrap, and there was a sign underneath. The sign said, "The only free cheese is in the trap."

That's what a lot of the people today don't realize. Traps come with all kinds of trappings, and one of the biggest traps is socialism. Hearing this will make some people furious. But I say this just for love. Because whenever people try to get something that they haven't earned, they're going to pay for it at some point. And they're going to pay for it very dearly. When they do, the payment comes in a way that they hadn't expected.

They go off peeping, like a little bird fallen out of its nest, saying, "I'm a victim, I'm a victim, I'm a victim, I'm a victim." They do that for an entire lifetime, peeping, "I'm a victim, I'm a victim." Who cares? They can take all the material goods they want from other people, because when this life is over, they have to leave it all behind. Then Soul comes back into a new body and starts all over again, maybe born into wealth, maybe into poverty. And if

that Soul is born into wealth, maybe It loses everything and becomes poor; or if that individual is poor,
he works his way up through life and becomes very
rich. But from one extreme to another, whether in
this life or another, the only free cheese is in the trap.

When people begin to realize this, then they have
realized a measure of truth.

People who understand truth understand love
and have love. These people are self-responsible. They
are strong. They are strong in and of themselves.
They go through the same hardships as other people,
but they are the ones with an inner strength. Life
will try to crush their spirit, but their strength comes
not from any kind of material goods or a wealthy
background. It is an inner strength. They love un-
conditionally. They love God because they know that
God loves them. And anyone who truly knows this
will find a great sense of freedom.

*People who
understand truth
understand love
and have love.*

GIFT OF FLOWERS

One day an ECKist in Germany decided that she
was going to invite a seventy-seven-year-old woman
to go with her on what she calls "a love adventure."
The woman who was doing the inviting was fifty-
three.

When she asked this older woman, "How would
you like to go on a love adventure?" the older woman's
eyes narrowed. She was looking at the younger
woman, wondering, *Has she lost her mind? Is she
OK?* The older woman had gone through a very hard
life; she had had many difficulties. The ECKist saw
that the best thing she could do for her friend was
something just for love.

Eventually the older woman saw the twinkle in
the ECKist's eyes. And when the older woman saw

the twinkle in her eyes, she said yes.

When they met for the adventure, the older woman brought a friend of hers along—just in case. She must have figured it didn't hurt to have somebody else along in case this ECKist was out of her mind.

The ECKist said, "Let's go to a restaurant in town. And before we go, we're going to have a rule: we're going to do something for love without expecting or wanting anyone to say thank you, or without anyone having any way of being able to pay us back." The ECKist, of course, was the only one in Eckankar. The other two women didn't know anything about ECK.

Those were the rules, and so the three women went to the restaurant. They ordered their meal. They had a good time talking about various things. They finished their meal, and as they were leaving, they looked at the next table where a young woman had been seated most of the time. She was very sad and seemed to be weighed down by some heavy burdens. As they went out the door, they stopped at the cashier and paid their bill. Then they said to the cashier, "We want to pay the bill for the young lady seated there too, just for the joy of giving. OK?" The cashier said, "I understand." So she took care of it, and they left.

They carried a feeling of love with them because the young woman never knew who to thank.

They carried a feeling of love with them because the young woman never knew who to thank.

Next the three women went to the open market where people sold flowers and vegetables. They went to a florist, bought some roses, and arranged them into a pretty bouquet. They said, "Let's give these flowers away if we can find someone who needs them." And as they were making up the bouquet, the Inner Master said to the ECKist, "Do you see that woman sitting on the side there watching you three arrange these roses? Offer her this bouquet." And so the ECKist took it straight over to the woman and said, "Would you like this?" The woman was very grateful and hugged the ECKist. She was smiling, and tears were in her eyes. It was very wonderful.

When the ECKist came back to the two other women, they said, "We would like to have that experience too." So they went back to the florist, got some more flowers, arranged them, and tried to give those flowers away so that they could get hugged by somebody, so that there would be tears and shining eyes.

The first person they tried to give the flowers to was a handicapped person in a wheelchair. The two women went up to her and said, "Here, would you like these flowers?" The woman said, "They're very lovely, but I've got too many things to carry, and I just can't carry roses with me." The two women felt bad. They sat down again with their flowers. And they looked here and they looked there, trying to find someone to give the roses to.

The ECKist said to them, "Remember our rule. Are we breaking our rule? We were just going to do this for love. Just for love, remember? And now you were trying to get somebody to hug you and to cry. That's not just for love anymore." And the two women said, "Ah, that's right. We didn't know quite how the rules work when we're actually playing this game." So the ECKist said, "Why don't we give them back to the florist and ask her to give them to somebody after we're gone?" So they took the bouquet back to the florist and asked her, "Would you give these to someone? Would you give these to someone who looks as if they need them?" The florist was an honest

So they took the bouquet back to the florist and asked her, "Would you give these to someone? Would you give these to someone who looks as if they need them?"

person; she would not put them back on the rack and resell them. So she said, "Sure," as if it was an everyday occurrence. And the three women learned a little about love, about how they couldn't give away their flowers expecting anything in return. How they had to give them away just for love.

SEMINAR TRAVEL

Sometimes on a Friday evening at a seminar I find it very difficult to communicate some of these ideas. Many of you have been traveling, many of you have gone through hardships to just get here.

Travel has all its little tricks and trials. It may have brought you right to the very edge of your patience, and when you finally get here, you sit in your seat, and you say, "Thank goodness, we made it. Now let's just sit here and go to sleep." So Friday night can be a very hard time to convey messages or ideas to people. But tonight it's easier. You are very receptive.

LOOKING FOR TRUTH

In the Eckankar Spiritual Center in Minneapolis, Minnesota, there is a lot of respect among the staff for each other. So one day, one of our editors, Tony, sees Carol, who works in RESA Services. She had been out sick, and so Tony asks Carol, "How are you doing?" And she says, "Fine. Almost back to normal."

"Oh," he says, teasing her. "And we were hoping for so much more."

This is very dry humor.

Carol often leads a discussion class at the Temple of ECK. During one of the Minnesota storms, she wondered if anybody would come to the book discussion class. Not too many people did, but surprisingly, one of the visitors was a guest from Paris. A lot of the local people couldn't make it, but this person made it all the way from Paris.

The young man explained what brought him. He said he had been in Paris and was searching for truth. There were things he wanted to know. He was looking for truth. So a spiritual traveler came to him, took him out of the body, and said, "Go to Minneapolis." And this young man, just on the strength of his experience of being taken out of the body by a spiritual traveler, came to Minneapolis, with no idea of what he's looking for except that he was to come. He even came in winter, so you know he's got to be sincere.

He was wandering around one of the suburbs, in Chanhassen, where the Temple of ECK is, and he saw the Temple all lit up. "That must be it," he said, because there's not too much else lit up. And when he got to the Temple, he found the ECKists in a very small class, having a book discussion.

They were talking about the very things that he wanted to know. He wanted to know about truth, and he was delighted to find others who were looking for the very same thing. So he stayed for the class. They even had their picture taken together.

He wanted to know about truth, and he was delighted to find others who were looking for the very same thing.

Before he left, the young man said, "Now I know there are others seeking such things too."

Eckankar is more than an organization, it's more than a bunch of little classes stretched around the world—here, there, and everywhere. It's a place where people who are looking and have found truth can be together. It's just that simple. This is the reason for the ECK seminars, so that people of like spiritual mind and heart can be together. To be with someone else who understands the ways of Divine

Spirit, someone else who understands, as a matter of the spiritual ABCs, the fact of karma and reincarnation.

BASIC SPIRITUAL PRINCIPLES

People in ECK don't walk on water; they don't float through the sky as some of the saints have been able to do through levitation. We make mistakes; we do the best we can. But by knowing basic spiritual principles, we find life to be much richer than it was before we found ECK.

The first principle is: Soul exists because God loves It. This means you exist because God loves you. Just knowing this gives a sense of freedom and joy to anyone who really knows what it means.

I try to bring out the esoteric side of the spiritual teachings, but I think some of the more necessary aspects are how to live and make it in this world. These are very stressful times for many people, if for no other reason than there are so many more people here.

On the farm, whenever the chicken barn was full of chickens, you could expect problems. When chickens are crowded, they get edgy. Chickens need their space. When the chicken barn didn't have quite as many chickens, there was more peace and quiet.

If one chicken flies, all chickens fly. That's a rule. And so you learn to go into the chicken barn very slowly and carefully. And so, too, the ECK Masters come into the consciousness of people who are new to truth very carefully and only by invitation. People are usually a bundle of fear, of one fear or another. Basically the inside of human beings is—not always but many times—like a barn full of chickens. Very fidgety, always in motion, always looking here and

We make mistakes; we do the best we can. But by knowing basic spiritual principles, we find life to be much richer than it was before we found ECK.

there. One noise, and they're all up against the far wall, standing on top of each other. The same as when people in a group find themselves with a problem.

GRATITUDE

A woman wondered about the importance of gratitude. She had heard this spoken of so often in the ECK teachings. She asked, "What's the point? What does gratitude do? Why have gratitude?"

Gratitude springs from a recognition of divine love. That's all. People who can show gratitude know and recognize God's love when it comes to them. But it made no sense to this woman.

Gratitude springs from a recognition of divine love. That's all.

Shortly after that, she had a dream. She was working in the Minneapolis area at the time. In the dream, she felt a beam, or a ray, of energy lift her above the bed. She didn't realize that this was the first step of Soul Travel. The Mahanta, the Living ECK Master had come to her to show her the importance of gratitude.

He lifted her a little above the bed, and for some reason which is very unlike her, she said, "Well, thank you very much, Mahanta. I can see my bed!" And she meant it from the bottom of her heart. A little thing like this. She went up a little higher, and she could see her apartment. She said, "Oh, Mahanta, thank you, I can see my apartment!" She could see it below her, and she had never felt this kind of gratitude.

When you have an inner experience like this, your perceptions also expand. They go far beyond the human senses, and there is a greater capacity for love and understanding. She was having a greater capacity for gratitude. But she didn't realize it at the moment.

Next she saw herself above some lakes, and then

she was above Minneapolis itself. "Thank you, thank you, Mahanta!" she said. "I can see Minneapolis!" She was up there in the sky. Pretty soon, she was above the clouds, then beyond the stars. Then, very quickly, almost like the snap of a finger, she came back into the body.

The woman realized that at every level she had said thank you with sincerity. She had said thank you from the bottom of her heart. This gave more love to take her to still a higher level and a greater viewpoint. Of what? Gratitude.

She learned the importance of gratitude through this experience. This experience of Soul Travel was not so she could have a Soul Travel experience. They are not given for that purpose. People misunderstand the idea of Soul Travel and dream travel; they think these are just things to delight the senses, to have a good time, to have something to brag about to friends later.

You learn very quickly that the experiences that the ECK Masters give you, like Soul Travel, are not for bragging about but to accomplish a spiritual goal.

You find that when you say, "I've had a Soul Travel experience," 99 percent of the people in the world are spiritually deaf and blind. They have no idea what you're talking about. And they don't like to hear you talking about it, because it upsets their own beliefs. They have had no experience with such spiritual things, so they feel uncomfortable. The only way they can feel comfortable is to make you be quiet. You learn very quickly that the experiences that the ECK Masters give you, like Soul Travel, are not for bragging about but to accomplish a spiritual goal.

In this case, the woman was to learn the importance of gratitude. She realized that one must acknowledge the gift from the bottom of one's heart. And this is basically, simply, just for love. You do it simply for love.

I have to go over these points repeatedly, because this is the essence of any truth. And that is simply: divine love. God loves you. And because God loves you, you can then love God in return.

But it takes people a long time to realize that once they understand the first half of the equation—that God loves them—the second part is that now they can love God in return.

> *God loves you. And because God loves you, you can then love God in return.*

SELF-RESPONSIBILITY

I find it interesting that the flu and viruses go rampant just at the holidays, usually right after Thanksgiving in the United States. Whenever there's a lot of food, it takes about two weeks, between Thanksgiving and Christmas, before people get very, very sick. They say, "It's a bug." And right after Christmas and New Year's, the virus strikes again, with a vengeance. "It's a bug," they say again. A very clean way of doing things, because it relieves a person of all responsibility for gluttony. It's not, "I ate too much" or "I overloaded myself and gave these viruses a good toehold." No, because if it's a bug, it's a bug. And that takes care of that. "I got good and sick, and then I got good and well. Boy, I hope it's better next year." Next year, it's pretty much the same old story.

I find it very interesting that often the virus gets a lot of help from the celebrants, from the people who love to eat during the holidays and pave the way for a lot of the illness that we take for granted.

People used to take old age for granted. Abraham Lincoln was old at the age of fifty, he said. I would like to think that at fifty I'm halfway through my life and I've got the other half to go. What changes people's perception on age and on health? Moving into a higher state of consciousness. In other words, when they move into a higher state of consciousness, they learn more about self-responsibility.

"I AM ALWAYS WITH YOU"

An ECKist got sick with the flu right around the time of the holidays. During her illness she got that lost feeling. When you're very sick, your defenses are down. She's had many experiences in ECK—she's a solid member of Eckankar. But despite her many experiences with the Light and Sound of God and with the ECK Masters, she suddenly began to cry.

"What have I learned from all these years in Eckankar?" she asked. "Haven't I learned anything?"

On the third day, she crawled out of bed, went to the bathroom, and while she was there, just as an afterthought, she got on the scale. And she looked down at the numbers, and she smiled in spite of herself, in spite of her sickness. Her weight had dropped below that impossible barrier; she hadn't been below that impossible barrier for two years. She smiled, and she felt a lot better.

She still had the flu, but she went back to bed. She felt a lot better. She said, "I got past the impassable barrier. I'm lighter!" Of course, she'd been sick, hadn't been eating much.

Suddenly there was a flash of blue light, and in the center of the blue light was pure white light.

She got into bed, and then with her eyes open, she saw this line of ECK Masters coming into her room. They filed past and looked at her. As they filed in, an incredible love came with them; and she began to cry because of joy and of love. All this time, her eyes were wide open.

Suddenly there was a flash of blue light, and in the center of the blue light was pure white light. A voice said, "Don't forget this." Trying to imprint on her, as the Masters do again and again: "I am always with you, my love is always with you, because we are both of God."

And so in closing, I too would like to say, I am always with you, and my love is with you. May the blessings be.

ECK Springtime Seminar, San Francisco, California, Friday, April 5, 1996

They went down to the river and chopped a hole in the ice. The boy's job was to herd the cattle down there every day and let them drink.

6

OUR SPIRITUAL WAKE-UP CALLS

hroughout most people's lives, there are turning points, or wake-up calls. These are very important in the spiritual life, because something significant happens.

Usually we're not so sure that this significant happening is for our good. In fact, we usually think something went wrong. We hang on to our old ways and our old thoughts, our old habits, hanging on because we know the past. It's comfortable. It may not be the best, but at least it's like an old friend. The future is unknown, a deep, black ocean that terrifies us.

These spiritual wake-up calls come sometimes in dreams, sometimes in symbols or daily events, occasionally from an ECK Master.

Most of us are people who like routine; we like things to stay exactly as they are. But if we keep going through our lives, doing things exactly as we've always done them, we're never going to move forward on the path to God. It can't happen. We're going to be exactly where we were, forever and ever. For those of you who understand the spiritual works, you know

Throughout most people's lives, there are turning points, or wake-up calls.

113

that this is impossible. You either go forward or you go backward, one or the other.

WE LIKE OUR ROUTINES

An ECKist wrote a letter to me. When he was a boy, he remembers his family moving from Iowa to Minnesota, to the Thief River Falls area. This was back in 1932, during the Depression. On March 1, the temperature was minus thirty-three degrees.

They had a herd of thirty cows, and the cows were mostly kept inside. The river froze; so the father and son went down to the river and cut a hole in the ice about thirty feet out, for the cows to drink from.

I hadn't noticed all the thirties in this story: 1932, minus thirty-three degrees, thirty cows, thirty feet out. Thirty is a number based on three, the creative element. The positive, the negative, and the neutral element, which are the creative force.

Anyway, they went down to the river and chopped a hole in the ice about thirty feet off the riverbank. The boy's job was to herd the cattle down there every day and let them drink. The cows would come down the bank, walk across the ice to the water hole, and drink. Then the boy would herd the cows back up to the barn. This all went very nicely until spring came, and the ice began to thaw.

The ice near the bank began to thaw first. Each day the cows would stand on the bank, looking at their water hole thirty feet out on the ice. Then they would walk through two feet of water, climb back on the ice, walk across the ice, and drink out of the hole. When it was time to go back to the barn, they would walk back across the ice, get to the edge of the ice, step into the water, walk through two feet of water, and climb back up on the bank. And this went on for days.

The boy couldn't believe it. He just watched these cows and how they had to drink out of that same water hole, even though they practically drowned getting there. As spring came along, more of the ice thawed, and the water got deeper.

The cows continued to make their trek out to the ice, which got more and more risky. Then one day, when the cows got to the river they saw that their water hole had sailed down the river, never to be seen again. Finally, the cows suddenly looked down at their feet and began to drink the water that was there.

Sometimes people are very much like this herd of cows.

Sometimes people are very much like this herd of cows. They have this habit of drinking water thirty feet off the riverbank, across the ice, and they insist on going there long after there is any need to do it. That is the nature of habits. Most people, if they had a choice, would always go out on the ice thirty feet to their water hole and drink there, even in summer. Seasons change, but that doesn't matter. They'll be out there at the same old water hole, doing the same old thing in the same old way, forever and ever, and complaining about it.

INTELLIGENT LIFE

You can almost hear the cows walking through the water, "Boy, this stuff is cold! Why isn't it like before, when we could just walk out there and not have to go through this cold stuff?" It's easy for us to laugh at dumb cows. We're not like that.

I sometimes listen to a certain radio commentator. And the only time I find it really hard to listen is when he starts saying that animals are stupid, because they can't add or subtract or understand any logical arguments. I don't think that necessarily makes them stupid. I've seen a lot of people who can add and subtract, but they usually do it to cheat someone else. Whenever this radio personality gets on this subject, I vote with my fingers and turn the radio off. Some people can be so narrow-minded about consciousness existing in anything other than a human being, particularly not in animals.

Animals do some marvelous things, not by instinct, but because they know things.

Animals do some marvelous things, not by instinct, but because they know things. They know that someone's in danger. A mother cat will rescue her kittens from a burning building, as Paul Harvey said on the news a couple of days ago. The mother cat's eyes were burned shut, and her paws were burned, but she kept going back in the building even as the firemen were trying to put the blaze out. The mother cat kept going in there, and she came out with something like four or five kittens. Instinct? I don't think so.

Our Spiritual Wake-Up Calls

Something is needed to wake up the herd. Usually it's the spring ice breakup, some kind of cataclysmic event, some kind of an ocean swell, a sea change, a catastrophe. This is what it takes to break the human mind of its habits and get it out of the rut, the rut of its spiritual life.

Back in the 1930s, during the Depression, in a slum in Birmingham, England, a young girl of five went to the school where her cousin would be getting out in an hour or so. She went there, and a golden light surrounded her. The interesting thing about this golden light, which happened to be a spiritual wake-up call for her, was that it sealed off the rest of the world. She couldn't hear or see anyone else. She was just in this beautiful golden light.

Imagine being a five year old and trying to explain to your peers what just happened, that you were caught in this golden light for half an hour and you couldn't see or hear anyone outside of this circle of light. She had a hard time doing this, and she soon learned not to try anymore.

Soul, when It comes to this earth in this lifetime, has made an agreement with Itself to accomplish some goal, to make some gain in spiritual unfoldment. By the time this woman was in her midthirties, she had studied Edgar Cayce and the Rosicrucians. She saw the ads that Paul Twitchell used to put in *Fate* magazine about Eckankar. But all this time she never got interested in Eckankar. She married an executive in the movie industry. She had a family of three children, a very busy social calendar, and a fast-moving life. She studied Astara and Theosophy, read the books of H. Rider Haggard and others. And in 1972, she saw a couple of UFOs. She joined three different branches of Buddhism.

Soul, when It comes to this earth in this lifetime, has made an agreement with Itself to accomplish some goal, to make some gain in spiritual unfoldment.

SPIRITUAL MEMORY LOSS

So this was her life. Then she wonders, *Why did it take me until 1994 to become a member of Eckankar?* She knew about Paul Twitchell and the ECK writings way back in the midsixties.

The answer is not that she was slow spiritually or anything on that order. The answer is that she had an agreement with herself before this lifetime to make a very thorough and broad study of all the different world religions and psychic groups, to read all different kinds of books to gain solid knowledge about the different ideas that exist about truth. This was her purpose.

When the wake-up call came via this golden light that surrounded her, it was the Light of God. The

Light was a reminder, saying, "OK, you've come out of the childhood years." Usually children from the age of two up to five or six remember past lives. Later they forget, simply because amnesia is also part of the deal. When children go to school and the social consciousness starts coming in, at this point it has been agreed that the memory of past lives is forgotten, total amnesia. The memory is totally gone; they forget everything.

This way, Soul begins with a clean slate. It doesn't harbor grudges from before. It doesn't fall into the old rut of wasting a life with unnecessary problems that belonged to last time, like getting into a duel.

Memory loss is beneficial to Soul's unfoldment. But somewhere along the line, Divine Spirit sends a wake-up call.

Memory loss is beneficial to Soul's unfoldment. But somewhere along the line, Divine Spirit sends a wake-up call. It comes through some of the workers in the spiritual hierarchy. And the spiritual wake-up call says, "OK, time to remember what you came here for."

Of course, the memory of a person's spiritual goal is never, or hardly ever, that clear. Most of you have gone through years and years of uncertainty, going from one religion to another, going from one interest in the occult to another, from philosophy to psychology, to any of these different subjects, even mathematics. Trying to understand the key to life and truth. And sometimes you make little gains here and there, but you back off at some point. Then you say, "There's got to be more." Something, some inner nudge, leaves you dissatisfied with the knowledge that you have gained up to this point. And some hidden thing inside your heart drives you on in your search for God and truth.

MEETING WITH AN ECK MASTER

This woman finally joined Eckankar in 1994, but before she did, she had an experience with the ECK Master Rebazar Tarzs. He was acting in the capacity of a wake-up call because she had been a spiritual student under him at some point in the past.

Often people find that an ECK Master who has been with them in the past is with them again in this lifetime. Sometimes it may be Gopal Das. He's a golden-haired individual often dressed in white. Or Lai Tsi, a Chinese ECK Master. Or Fubbi Quantz, the abbot of the Katsupari Monastery in the mountains of northern Tibet. These people come to seekers in their dreams, even as Rebazar Tarzs did to this woman, before she actually knew that much about him. These Masters come.

People meet the ECK Masters often before they have any knowledge of Eckankar at all. There are critics of Eckankar who say there are no ECK Masters, that they are all figments of someone's imagination. And yet, they're there. There are the testimonials of people who have met these Masters long before they knew there was any connection between them and the path of ECK.

AWAKENING PAST CONNECTIONS

Very often, there is a connection through the eyes. All of a sudden two people look into each other's eyes—perhaps lovers—and suddenly there is the knowingness of having met a very old, dear friend. Life or nature follows its course, and the people get married or form a friendship.

But sometimes, this wake-up call is of a different kind. It awakens a past memory tied to not-so-favorable circumstances.

Often people find that an ECK Master who has been with them in the past is with them again in this lifetime.

A woman who was a dental hygienist was going from temporary job to temporary job. Each office she worked in, she was very careful to please the dentist—trying to keep harmony at the office, trying to work with the patients so that everything would be in good shape after she left, so the patients would still like the doctor.

One day a patient came in for an appointment. As the ECKist began assembling her cleaning instruments, ready to clean the teeth of this individual, she looked down into the woman's eyes for the first time. The patient jumped up suddenly, saying, "I know what you're going to do, and you're not going to do it. I'm getting out of here." And the patient ran out of the office.

One of your typical days in a dentist's office.

The dental hygienist was concerned because this might reflect on her skills. The doctor wouldn't be very happy about it. He was in the next room, and it was very easy to hear the woman's screaming.

The dental hygienist decided that maybe she had injured this woman in a past life. But actually, the patient had injured the dental hygienist. And when she looked in the hygienist's eyes, she figured this was a good time for retribution. But she didn't want any part of it. I know some of you feel you're working out past-life problems with someone in the dentist's office. I've felt that way myself.

Later the ECKist realized that, as that patient left, a weight lifted from her own heart, a heavy weight she hadn't known was there.

But things turned out very nicely. The hygienist never went back to that office. In a week's time she had a new job, a permanent job, at a good office.

Later the ECKist realized that, as that patient left, a weight lifted from her own heart, a heavy weight she hadn't known was there. It was replaced with joy, which is a strange thing to have happen after you have an experience of this sort. Something had changed. It was a wake-up call, and it awakened her to a spiritual blessing from God.

A LESSON IN COURAGE

Another time, the same woman had stomach pains. They were to teach her courage.

She went to a doctor who said, "I'm going to put this fiber-optic device all the way down your throat, and I'm going to look down there. It's no problem. People go through it all the time." As he turned his back to get his instruments ready, the woman began to shake.

Her body began to shake more and more violently, and she started crying. She was terrified. The doctor asked, "What's the matter?" But the woman couldn't tell him. She was so upset, just a basket case emotionally, that the doctor finally said, "In this condition, I can't take the responsibility for doing this procedure on you. We'll have to do it another time."

Suddenly it dawned on this woman that the stomach pain had been a wake-up call for her. The Mahanta, the Living ECK Master was giving her an opportunity to face something, to gain courage in a new way. Courage to face something that she had been afraid to face in the past. He had set up this whole elaborate thing, the stomach pain and all kinds of gastric distress, so that she could have this experience and face her fear. And she had almost thrown the experience away.

Just like that she caught herself. She realized this was a spiritual experience. It wasn't some doctor trying to balance some karmic wrongdoing from the past that she had done to him. The woman realized she had what she calls a "golden contract with the

Just like that she caught herself. She realized this was a spiritual experience.

Mahanta," to lead her into situations that are for her spiritual understanding. And just like that, she settled down on the examining table, quietly smiling to herself. "It's OK," she told the doctor. "I'm fine now; you can go ahead with the procedure." The doctor looked at her carefully. "What happened to you?" he asked, concerned because she was now absolutely calm.

But just then the assistant came in and gave her the anesthetic, saying, "This is going to burn a little." "Don't worry," she said, "it's all fine now." Then they hooked her up to an IV. After that everything was OK.

She had faced herself. She had moved forward spiritually because she had had the courage to face her fears. Because she had remembered the golden contract she had with the Mahanta. The stomach pains were a wake-up call.

Our spiritual wake-up calls can also be for the benefit of other people.

PLAYERS IN THE SPIRITUAL DRAMA

Our spiritual wake-up calls can also be for the benefit of other people. You become a player in someone else's spiritual unfoldment, one of many possibilities that occur as the spiritual drama of life unfolds.

It's almost as if a master weaver, with thousands of colored threads, is putting all these threads together and creating an exquisite design. It's one of a kind. There's no other design like it anywhere on earth. All the little threads of other people and their actions, our actions, our feelings, and everything else are all woven together in such intricate detail—with such care and with such beauty—for one reason. To uplift the individuals concerned.

An ECKist and her husband had made some money, and they decided to put a new window in the front of their house. The day after the window was installed, they heard this enormous crack. They ran to the front of their home. There they saw that the window had shattered into thousands of pieces. So they got into their car and drove to the window-installer's office.

The window shattering was a wake-up call for someone else, but they were the players — the husband and wife.

So they drove to the place where they bought the window. At the counter, being waited on, are two women and a three-year-old girl. The little girl happened to be retarded.

As soon as the wife walked in the door, the little girl opened her arms as if to say, "Pick me up, hug me. I trust you. I like you." This was very rare. The mother looked down at her daughter and couldn't understand why this little girl would suddenly open her heart to an absolute stranger. So the wife picked up the little girl and held her. Eventually, the girl got restless. The wife put her down, but the girl would always come back to the wife. The wife would pick her up again, pat her on the back, and just hold her.

A little bit later, the mother of the little girl went outside to the car to wait while the other woman finished their business. The husband and the wife finished their business, too, and went out to the car. But as they got into their car, the wife said to her husband, "Just a minute, I've got to do something."

She got out of the car, walked over to the car with the little girl, and said to the mother, "You asked me earlier what I had done that made your daughter quiet. When I held her, I sang HU quietly in her ear."

And the mother said, "What is HU?"

"It is an ancient name for God. If your daughter

You asked me earlier what I had done that made your daughter quiet. When I held her, I sang HU quietly in her ear.

is ever upset and you want to quiet her, to make her feel that she is whole and loved, sing or say this word very softly to her."

When the ECKist said this, the woman in the car said, "You are a person of God. That's why she went to you."

The wake-up call in this story was the window shattering, which caused the couple to be at the counter when the two women and the young girl were there. But the wake-up call was for the mother of the little girl. It was HU. HU was brought into her life through the love and acceptance of her three-year-old daughter.

These are just examples of how our spiritual wake-up calls come.

BECOMING SPIRITUALLY ALERT

A husband was going out the door. It's near midnight, he has to get to work for the midnight shift. As he's going out the door, his wife says, "Would you take the garbage out? And he says, "Sure."

In one hand he has a bag full of things to take to work. In the other hand is the garbage. But as he passes the trash can, he throws in his work bag. Then he stops, realizing what he's just done. When you're working the night shift like this, it can be very hard to function right.

As he goes to the trash can to pull out his work bag and throw away the garbage, he wonders, *What is this about?* Because this was a wake-up call for him.

When he got to work, his manager came up to him and told him that she has assigned him to Saturday morning plus four nights that week. Did he like it or didn't he? she wants to know.

But the wake-up call was for the mother of the little girl. It was HU.

The man remembered that a few weeks earlier, there had been a general meeting where the manager had told the people working for her, "When I give an order and you don't obey it immediately, that's insubordination, grounds for being fired on the spot." So during this conversation, it almost seemed as if the manager was trying to push this man into getting himself fired. It seemed as if she was looking for any excuse to fire him for insubordination. But he looked at the schedule, and he said, "That's fine. It's perfectly fine with me."

That's when he realized that the incident with his work bag had been a wake-up call for him. Because as he was throwing it into the trash, it crossed his mind that that night he could be throwing away his job. Because that had happened, he was very alert. He had it in his consciousness that the Mahanta, the Living ECK Master was trying to get a message across to him. And he had the awareness to listen.

The Mahanta, the Living ECK Master was trying to get a message across to him. And he had the awareness to listen.

His wife had wanted to quit her job for some time, but he was against it. She said, "With this job, I can never get to the ECK Worship Service, and I would love to go." But he always told her, "No, the commute to another job would be too long." But when he got this ultimatum at work, he suddenly thought it was a good idea to support his wife. Maybe she could find a better job with better pay, one where she could also go to the ECK Worship Service. Soon a new job with better pay did come along. A double blessing. This is what the wake-up call of throwing the wrong bag, his business materials, into the trash was all about.

LEAP OF FAITH

These are the sort of things that happen in people's lives all the time, in one way or another. Our wake-up calls are spiritual wake-up calls. But when they happen, most people don't recognize them until it's too late. What we're trying to offer you in Eckankar is the ability to increase your awareness of these things. You learn this through the Spiritual Exercises of ECK. If you do this simple discipline of the spiritual exercises every day, it can give you greater awareness of how God's love is flowing to you every minute, trying to lead you into a greater and better life.

When people don't understand that a change is for their own good, they usually shut the door to the blessings of God—just because it is change. And then they complain that life treats them so unfairly.

The people who turn down the most opportunities are often those who complain most about the unfairness of life. It's an interesting thing. If you were to mention to them that they have turned down one opportunity after another, they would just say, "That wasn't an opportunity. What's the matter with you?" From their viewpoint, it's not.

Following Divine Spirit always requires a leap of faith.

When people don't under- stand that a change is for their own good, they usually shut the door to the blessings of God—just because it is change.

ATTITUDE OF TRUST

A certain ECKist has a very positive attitude toward most things that happen in his life. One time he had a two-part dream. In the dream he was approached by a group of thugs looking for a fight, so he used the dream as an experiment. He sang HU, took off his coat, handed it to them, and left the scene unharmed. Not long after, the dream repeated. This time he thought, *I'm tired of being a rug for thugs. I'm going to fight.* And he fought. They beat him up, pulled off his coat, and left him in the dust. After the second part, he said to himself, "So that's the other side of the experiment. I think I'll sing HU every time." So this is his attitude; he's come to trust HU.

So one day, a series of wake-up calls came to this person. As he was opening a bottle of hair oil, it slipped out of his hands, and even as it was going through the air toward the rug and the floor, he could see it breaking on the floor and splashing all over the rug.

But suddenly the bottle landed right side up, without a spill or a break. It was just perfect. This was the first of his wake-up calls.

The second wake-up call came via a container of rice. As he was putting the container on the table, he missed the edge. His hand couldn't move fast enough to catch the container, and he saw it going over the edge of the table, hitting the floor, and all those nice little pieces of rice going all over. *Big time mess,* the guy thought. What happens? This guy lives well. The container flipped, landed upright on the chair, and didn't spill any rice to speak of.

Aah, isn't that wonderful, the man thought. *No mess!*

Not long after these two wake-up calls, the man began having problems with an old knee injury that forced him to seek medical attention. He had just gotten a new job that required a lot of physical activity, and this was not the time for his knee to go out. But instead of being despondent about this old knee injury, he knew that no matter how things turned out, it was going to be for his spiritual good.

He knew this because of the wake-up calls: the hair oil and the container of rice. It wasn't important what happened to the bottle, the container of rice,

But suddenly the bottle landed right side up, without a spill or a break. It was just perfect. This was the first of his wake-up calls.

or to his knee, he realized. What was important was his attitude about what would come of all this. He knew that the best possible thing for his spiritual unfoldment would happen because this is the agreement he has with life.

THE REALITY OF HU

A woman in a busy office saw how much pressure her manager was under. One day she asked the manager, "How do you deal with all this pressure? What do you do?"

The manager is an ECKist. When she heard the question, she sat there for a moment trying to think of an answer. She had never mentioned Eckankar or ECK to any of the people on her staff. But the woman was persistent. She asked, "Do you meditate?" So this was the opening. The ECKist said, "I listen to a HU tape, and I sing HU. Would you like to borrow the HU tape?" "Yes, I'd very much like to," said the coworker, and she borrowed the audiocassette for two weeks.

During this time, the ECKist got a large poster of the Temple of ECK in Chanhassen. She put it up on her wall at work. Shortly after, the coworker came into the manager's office, went straight to the poster on the wall, and asked, "What is this? What is this place?"

"That is the Temple of ECK; it's in Minnesota," the ECKist explained.

The woman said, "Just a minute." She went to her own desk and brought back a blue envelope from the Eckankar Spiritual Center in Minneapolis.

"Is this envelope connected with that picture?"

"Why, yes, it's the same place. ECK and Eckankar, same place," the ECKist said.

He knew that the best possible thing for his spiritual unfoldment would happen because this is the agreement he has with life.

The coworker explained, "I was out one day, and I saw a poster with cards tucked into it. I sent one in, and they sent me this information." This happened after she had heard about HU. The coworker didn't realize that HU, the poster and card about Eckankar, and the poster of the Temple of ECK were all from the same place. These were her wake-up calls.

Over the next few months, the ECKist noticed some remarkable changes happening in her coworker. This coworker had a lot of problems, but whenever she came to talk the ECKist simply listened. She just listened; she gave a sympathetic ear. But as the months passed, it became apparent that a change was taking place in the life of the coworker. She began talking about plans to relocate from Iowa to Arizona. She began making arrangements to move. She started to sell things, to get her affairs in order. Gradually, things began to change.

This coworker had a lot of problems, but whenever she came to talk the ECKist simply listened.

The ECKist sat back watching all this very quietly, never saying a word, never interfering, never having to talk to her about ECK because this woman had made her own connection. After the initial contact with HU, Divine Spirit had lined up all these wake-up calls for her.

One of the things the coworker had to sell before she left was a piano. One day, she left work to see a woman who wanted to buy the piano.

While the coworker was at this woman's house, she noticed a framed prayer on the wall. She looked at it very carefully. It was the same prayer that a beloved aunt and uncle had given her when she was seven years old. But she had lost track of her framed prayer after she divorced her first husband. He knew that this prayer meant so very much to her. So, very spitefully, he took it to a yard sale and gave it away. Somebody who would do that with something so precious to someone else, you have to say, "There are certainly all kinds of creatures in this world: those who live outside of the trash can and those who live inside, at the very bottom."

The coworker asked the woman, "May I take that off the wall?" and the woman said, "Sure, go ahead." As she turned the frame over, she saw on the back an inscription to herself. Of course, she began crying.

The woman who was buying the piano had no idea what was going on: A stranger walks into her house to sell her a piano and then begins crying. The coworker explained to the woman, "That's the prayer that my aunt and uncle gave to me when I was seven," and she explained about how her ex-husband had given it away at a yard sale just to hurt her as much as he could.

The prayer was very interesting: "O angel of God, my guardian dear, to whom God's love commits me here. Ever this day be at my side to light, to guard, to rule and guide." Just a beautiful prayer. The framed prayer reminded her of that age where the memories of past lives were just beginning to be shut out so that she could start living this life with a fresh, clean slate.

Our spiritual wake-up calls sometimes come through dreams.

MESSAGE IN A DREAM

Our spiritual wake-up calls sometimes come through dreams. The mother of a family began having dreams of a cream-colored puppy with brown spots. These dreams about the cream-colored puppy with the brown spots were her wake-up call, the symbol that would awaken her consciousness to begin looking and searching. In the dream, the Mahanta, the Inner Master, told her, "This dog is important because it will teach you and your family about love."

The family had two sons, and they were looking for a dog for the kids. They had one dog already, a four-year-old dog, but they wanted a second.

First, the woman went to the animal shelter, and she looked at all the dogs. None of the dogs there fit the description of the dog in her dreams. Soon after that, she had a dream of an Australian shepherd, but that dog never showed up either. Then she decided to go to a boarding and rescue kennel nearby.

It was winter, and she had to go up a steep hill to get to the kennel. But her car wouldn't climb the hill. After several tries, she finally parked her car at the bottom of the hill, saying to herself, "Ah, forget it, it's too slippery, too treacherous to try to get up there." As she was sitting in the car at the foot of this hill, she saw a woman nearby. She went up to the woman and asked, "Do you know about that kennel up there?" The woman said, "Oh yes, you have got to go up there."

"By the way, have you seen a cream dog with brown spots anywhere?" the woman asked. "It's missing."

This caught the woman's attention because it was her wake-up call from the dream, but at the time she didn't recognize it as such. It appeared the woman who lived at the foot of the hill had her dream dog. It had been missing for a couple of hours. She was just going out to look for the dog when the ECKist had driven up.

The woman said, "I'm going to drive up to the kennel to ask if they've seen my dog. If you want to, we can go together." The ECKist said, "OK," even though she was still nervous about the hill because it was so treacherous.

This caught the woman's attention because it was her wake-up call from the dream, but at the time she didn't recognize it as such.

They arrived at the kennel safely, and while the ECKist was there, she saw an older dog: a beagle mix, white with black spots, pretty close to the dog in her dream. As she looked at the dog, it seemed familiar. It was Peekhole, a dog they had given away nine years earlier because the dog was hyperactive and very destructive. It even seemed to be a little crazy. The family had given Peekhole to what they thought was a good home, but apparently the dog couldn't give up its habits or it had some other problem so it had ended up here in this boarding and rescue kennel.

The woman went home and told her family, "You know, I saw Peekhole." The family then decided that the only right thing to do was to go and see their old friend. They even considered taking the dog home again, but the dog hadn't lost any of its wild and crazy behavior even after nine years. It was definitely not a dog for young kids.

"Don't take this dog back because you feel guilty," the woman at the kennel told the family. The ECKist thought, *That's a principle in the ECK teachings too.* Feelings of guilt often trap you into doing things that you would rather not do. "No, we decided against taking Peekhole back," the family said. The woman at the kennel said, "I wouldn't have given you the dog anyway, because you would have only taken her because of guilt. Even if no one ever adopts her, she'll always have a place here."

Not long after, the family went back to the shelter. The mother had heard about a white dog with brown spots. As soon as they arrived, a white dog with brown spots appeared. It growled at the children then immediately got in a fight with the family's four-year old dog. Immediate disqualification; the

Feelings of guilt often trap you into doing things that you would rather not do.

family knew that dog wouldn't work.

But the person at the shelter said, "Hey, look at this little shepherd-terrier mix." It was a little puppy. The family fell in love with this little puppy right away. It wasn't white with little brown spots at all. It looked entirely different. But they fell in love with this little dog.

This little dog has brought them a lot of happiness and a lot of love, as the dream promised. The Mahanta had told the woman, "This dog will teach you and your family about love."

The woman realized that the search for the white dog with brown spots had led her to the puppy that the family loves so much.

FINDING TRUTH IS A PROCESS

Why does Divine Spirit work indirectly like this? Why didn't It just show the woman the little shepherd-terrier mix in the dream? Because sometimes the reason for living here is not just to get results. It is to go through the process of getting the results.

Sometimes the reason for living here is not just to get results. It is to go through the process of getting the results.

Why have truth handed to you on a platter? It wouldn't mean anything to you. But now, the whole family appreciates the little puppy because they had to sacrifice and search for him, and they came to so many dead ends with other dogs, even finding the old dog that they had given away nine years earlier. The ECK set it up this way so that they would go through the exquisite joy of sacrifice and effort. Because unless they did, they would not appreciate the gift.

I hope in some way I've given you a sense of what to look for in your own life and also an understanding of why these wake-up calls come when they do. They sometimes come indirectly, sometimes very directly. Don't ever discount the experiences that you went through coming to a certain stage in your life as a result of a certain wake-up call. Because the wake-up call is from the Holy Spirit. It is meant for your spiritual unfoldment.

ECK Springtime Seminar, San Francisco, California, Saturday, April 6, 1996

In this way, the cartoonists are working as servants of God. They're putting spiritual truths in front of people in ways that people can accept.

7

A Servant of God

*O*ne of my favorite cartoons when I was young was *Prince Valiant*. Cartoonists back in the fifties and sixties had very good imaginations, and some of the best cartoons came from that time. Comic books now are so heavy and dark and unimaginative; they just drain the spirit.

My daughter's been sending me *Prince Valiant* cartoons by John Cullen Murphy every month or two, and this morning I read a very interesting episode.

Cause and Effect

Prince Valiant, his son, Prince Arn, and others find themselves on the Island of Crippling Foresight. This fits in very well with the topic of spiritual amnesia that occurs when Soul comes to the earth plane. Before each of you comes here, you have an agreement to forget your past lives—simply because it makes a clean sweep and allows you to move forward spiritually.

There is wonderful insight in this *Prince Valiant* cartoon. The caretaker who meets Prince Valiant and his party tells them that on this Island of Crippling Foresight, "We have the misfortune of knowing

Spiritual amnesia occurs when Soul comes to the earth plane.

all the consequences of any of our actions."

Prince Valiant and his party look over to the side where the caretaker points to a man sitting down. Behind him on a little rocky ledge sits another man in the first man's shadow.

The caretaker explains that the man over there would like to move out of the sun, but he knows that if he does he will deprive the other man of his shade. The first man knows the second man is an irritable fellow and that he will then go home and become angry at his wife. She will leave him, and a savage war will erupt between their families. So the man stays in the sun. Just an ordinary little tiff between a couple starts a war.

Then Prince Arn asks why the second man doesn't just move.

The caretaker replies that the man may be irritable, but he's not a bad man. He knows that if the first man leaves, he will buy a ball for his daughter. A year later the ball will roll in front of a charging horse, and the girl will chase the ball. Here the caretaker shudders. He tries to explain the consequences of everything that happens.

Given enough time even the smallest actions can cause enormous effects.

Then there's an image of someone planting a little tree. On the other side there's a little hut with a shed attached to it. Snow is on it, and Prince Valiant, the caretaker, and Prince Arn are like giants standing and looking through this misty veil. The caretaker explains that given enough time even the smallest actions can cause enormous effects. He goes on to say that if we plant a tree in Cathay it may later yield a thunderstorm in Gaul. He asks which of us knows what our children or our grandchildren may do in the world. "What would you do if you knew in advance?" he concludes. Next week, the answer.

Spiritual Amnesia

Pretty spiritual stuff for the Sunday comics. In this way, the cartoonists are working as servants of God. They're putting spiritual truths in front of people in ways that people can accept. Even if people don't really accept it consciously, they have an unconscious knowing that what they're reading is true.

It's almost frightening for some people. Because part of the amnesia that people take on when they come here gives them almost an innocence. They don't want to believe in any kind of cause and effect because it puts responsibility on them. And since they don't know what they're doing — and never have — that's a fearful thing. Some of these messages coming through from cartoonists like this are inspired by the spiritual hierarchy. The message of truth keeps coming out into the world in ways that people can accept.

A Time of Increasing Responsibility

I'd like to mention a few things about my health. Thank you to those who sent information about different health products and methods of healing over the last few years.

My health is getting better, but I am still very, very weak. It takes a full day to get my energy up to come out here and look healthy and strong.

A valuable thing I have learned during this time is that the car accident in 1991 was a very significant turning point that I had agreed to before. It was to change the way we do things in ECK in the future. I won't get into that now. We do as much as we can.

It's a time of increasing responsibility for those of you who have developed and become strong in ECK. You're effective in telling other people about

It's a time of increasing responsibility for those of you who have developed and become strong in ECK.

HU and the teachings of ECK because you're right there—at home, in the workplace, with your friends. You're much more effective than any one person, such as myself, could ever be.

This path is not necessarily one where we have multitudes of people. The point is whoever is in ECK is going to have the best possible chance of spiritual unfoldment that is available on earth today. The changes we make are designed to allow you to help more. I think this is spiritually healthy for everyone.

The auto accident set up a chain of events that weakened my immune system. It threw off the chemistry in my body very subtly while I had all my attention on doing things for ECK and just moving forward. When my chemistry changed from alkaline to more acidic, some of the beneficial bacteria transmuted to harmful bacteria. They're often of the same family, the good and the bad. It just depends upon the environment, the body chemistry.

This chemistry change also opened a door for parasites as I traveled. I took a number of different medicines and finally got very good help from homeopathic medicine. We got the laboratory tests done, and the harmful parasites are finally gone.

The human condition believes that our way is the way, whether it's religion, medicine, or anything else.

When I told him the results, the earlier doctor I went to said, "Well, it must be a coincidence." I always get a kick out of that. The human condition believes that *our* way is *the* way, whether it's religion, medicine, or anything else. Our way is it. Any other way, if it works, must be coincidence. Human nature is really a lot of fun.

PARTNERSHIP IN HEALING

I can't tell you what medical sources to go to. But I found several practitioners who are very good at muscle testing, which is a part of Applied Kinesiology.

This is a very good diagnostic tool in the hands of a competent practitioner. I can't tell you who's capable and who's not because, as with many other things, some days a health practitioner is on and some days he's off. Even if you send a test sample to a lab, some days the lab catches the problem, some days it doesn't.

The bottom line is that those of you who are interested in your own health have to take responsibility for it. You are the one who has a contract with a doctor. You allow the doctor to go just as far as you feel comfortable and not one step farther, no matter what they say. Literally, you're taking your life in your own hands.

Sometimes even the most renowned practitioners in any healing field goof up; they make mistakes. Why? Because they're human. But the responsibility for your health is your own. You may even find the very best doctors through your inner side, through intuition.

You may even find the very best doctors through your inner side, through intuition.

As long as the doctor has respect for you, then you probably will have respect for the doctor. But as soon as he starts talking down to you like a child, like you're stupid, that's usually a clue to start looking for a new doctor. Because that doctor has taken you as far as he can. You may have to go to several doctors to find out what's actually wrong and how to find better health.

This is what I'm doing. I'm telling you this, while trying not to get very pedantic about which doctor to go to, what form of healing to follow. I just thought I'd mention my own experience here for those of you who are looking for help with allergies or any other health condition. Know that there is a way to move forward, that these healers are servants of God too. But this is earth, and it's an imperfect world.

The healing comes from a divine source just as long as the practitioner does not forget that he or she is an instrument for Divine Spirit in healing. As long as a healer does not get such a big head as to think that he is the one doing the healing, you're in good hands.

WAVES OF HU

One of the ECKists found herself in a hospital for emergency surgery. After the operation, she remembered what had happened to her as she went under sedation.

She was suddenly among waves, great blue waves of an immense kind.

She was suddenly among waves, great blue waves of an immense kind. She knew that these waves were the ECK, which is the Holy Spirit, the Voice of God which moves between God and the worlds of creation. The Light and the Sound of God were with her as she was in this experience.

As the waves rolled, she noticed there was order, not chaos. She said this was not God, the Sugmad, or the Ocean of Love and Mercy. It was the holy Sound of HU, or the Holy Spirit, the ECK Itself moving between God and the lower worlds.

Now the choice was hers—to stay in her body or go. She asked the Mahanta, "What should I do?" The question was very interesting because she said, "What should I *do?*" The Inner Master did not say, "Do this" or "Do that." He said, "Be the HU." Then she realized that the spiritual law for being a servant of God is not about doing, but about being.

And she was carried along on this blue-gray wave, clear and brilliant. The sound was sweet and soft, almost like an echo, but it carried her closer to the heart of God.

Lost and Found

An African ECKist came back from an ECK event late one night. In this part of Africa they live in compounds for safety. He wanted to get in quietly so he wouldn't wake his neighbors in the compound.

By the time he got inside, he discovered he had lost his gold-plated ᛖ pin.

This upset him very much, but since it was too dark to go outside and look for it, he determined to get up early the next morning and search for the pin.

Next morning he went outside and started looking for the ᛖ pin. But he couldn't find it. In Africa it's difficult to replace something like an ᛖ pin. There is a long delay in ordering and shipping, and packages often get stolen or lost in the mail. So the man began scolding himself. "Why did I lose it?" he said. "People won't respect me because now they won't see the pin." He worried as he walked back and forth between the compound walls to the apartments where he lived.

Suddenly it struck him: *As a servant of God, it won't make any difference what I wear—such as an ᛖ pin—it's what I am and how I act. With or without the ᛖ pin, I'm still an ECKist. People will respect me for the life I lead, not for a pin I wear.*

He had just gained this insight, and he was willing to let the pin go. He was willing to say, "OK, I made a mistake last night, I lost it, it's gone. Forget about it."

Just then, two women passed by. "Can we help you?" they asked the man.

He said, "I've lost a little pin, and I'm looking for it. I just can't find it."

Suddenly the sunlight hit the ground just right, and one of the women said, "Well, it's right there!"

As a servant of God, it won't make any difference what I wear—such as an ᛖ pin—it's what I am and how I act.

It was an area he had been over repeatedly. But there it lay, glinting in the sunshine. He thanked the women from the bottom of his heart.

The man got the pin back, but more importantly he had received a lesson about what it really means to be a servant of God. It doesn't require wearing a pin. It requires wearing your beliefs in your heart, because other people can read them there.

It requires wearing your beliefs in your heart, because other people can read them there.

HU Is Real

Many of the people who are more mature Souls, who have been around the lower worlds a long time, who have more experience, often find themselves in the healing fields in one way or another. Now all mature Souls are not necessarily in one of the healing fields, nor are all those outside those fields immature Souls. But a lot of Souls who are mature go into the healing fields because they want to be of service to life. They want to be a servant of God.

One day an ECKist who is a nurse at a home health agency was sharing with two other supervisors a way to overcome stress. There's a lot of stress involved with that line of work. "I simply sing HU," the ECKist said.

A little later, there was a general staff meeting, and the administrator asked for ideas on how to reduce negativity and make things go better. The stress was unbelievable, the people were out of focus, and the administrator wanted help with this. So the ECKist again said, "Well, there's HU." "OK," said the administrator, "we'll put this on the list along with all the other ways we can reduce negativity, stay in focus, and reduce stress."

After the staff meeting, the administrator got a

call from a very unpleasant client. She always had problems with this client. The administrator—knowing nothing about HU, this ancient name for God—spent the phone call listening to the client and all the time singing, "HU-U-U-U-U" quietly to herself. She did this for fifteen minutes. When she hung up, she talked about this to the supervisor. "You know, it works," she said. "And you know, he isn't such a bad guy after all. I kind of like him."

Singing a holy name for God as powerful as HU changes us—it doesn't change the other person, but it changes ourselves. Suddenly the administrator found that the difficult client had a valid point of view. She could put herself in his shoes and understand what he was saying and feeling. And as she came to understand him, she began to like him, at least a little bit.

Stress often comes in waves. When another particularly stressful time hit the agency, the ECKist was talking to another supervisor who had been at the staff meeting but now was really having a hard time. The ECKist said, "Have you forgotten to use HU?" The other woman said, "I don't use it because it doesn't work for me."

The ECKist had been reading Mary Carroll Moore's book *Turning Points: How to Handle Change in Your Life,* and she was discussing the book at work and working with some of the ideas that Mary had spoken of. Two of the supervisors were getting interested, so finally the woman who said HU didn't work for her said, "You know, that book sounds interesting. Could you bring it so I could read it?"

When the nursing supervisor opened the book, it opened right to a spiritual exercise that mentioned the word *HU.*

Singing a holy name for God as powerful as HU changes us—it doesn't change the other person, but it changes ourselves.

"Here's HU!" she exclaimed. "I thought you made it up!"

The word lost its power for her because she had been thinking, *That woman made up this word just to make everybody feel good, but I'm too smart for that.* From that point on, HU wouldn't work for her because she had thrown up mental blocks. But this is an authentic word of God: HU.

She read Mary's book, and she liked it. Soon others in the agency said they would like to read *Turning Points,* and this supervisor said she might even get another copy of the book herself to read again.

Many of you in ECK are now able to share the strength you have gained through the teachings of ECK. You're able to share this strength through your writings, your talks, and mainly through your being. Not only through what you do, but through what you are.

You now share the strength you have gained through the teachings of ECK, not only through what you do, but through what you are.

Life between Lives

I want to mention a book called *Journey of Souls* by Dr. Michael Newton. He's a doctor in California, and to the best of my knowledge, he is not a member of ECK at this time. The book is published by Llewellyn Publications of St. Paul, Minnesota.

As it says on the cover, this book is about case studies of life between lives. I think Dr. Newton has done some groundbreaking work here. He's a state certified master hypnotherapist, and he studies what Souls do between lives. The book is very good in many ways, but this is not the final word on certain aspects of the spiritual teachings.

I want to mention a few things that he doesn't seem to know or understand. When he looks at light, he's looking at it as a lower-world phenomenon, and down there things are a little jumbled.

Between each plane—for instance, between the Physical and the Astral Plane—there is a dark zone. It's to separate the people who are on the Physical Plane from the activities of those on the Astral Plane. And the barrier works in most cases. There's also a barrier between each one of the other planes.

Then there is a huge zone called Yreka, which is a black, almost impenetrable zone between the lower worlds and the higher worlds of pure Spirit. This zone appears between the high Mental worlds and the Soul Plane. None of the people the doctor has in his case histories have gone beyond that last zone. As the colors approach the higher worlds and get closer to that zone, they become darker in hue.

He thinks the light of the most immature Souls is white. And as the Souls mature, the light changes to yellow, pink, gold, blue, violet, and then into a dark purple.

What he also doesn't understand is that each plane, including the physical, has the whole spectrum, the whole rainbow, of colors. The Astral Plane also runs from white all the way to purple, as do the other lower planes. So there isn't a real parallel between the light that a Soul emits in his experience and the spiritual unfoldment of that individual.

There is a different, higher law that applies. Because once you get to the Soul Plane, you find that the light of Soul is a soft, white-golden light. In the lower worlds, the doctor sees the light going from lighter to darker. But in the pure spiritual worlds—beyond the lower worlds—it goes from light to even lighter. And the closer you get to the heart of God, it becomes a brighter, clearer, brilliant light. You can't really talk about it because it's beyond the scope

The closer you get to the heart of God, it becomes a brighter, clearer, brilliant light.

of the mind and language. If you read the book with an understanding of this, it will help.

AS ABOVE, SO BELOW

Be aware that the doctor is usually working with Souls who leave earth, come to an intermediate stage between lives, and are sent back to earth again. The ones who leave earth, the ones who have a higher nature, he never sees. They are the least likely people to come and consult him for help to get their lives together. So he has very few case histories of people who are in the higher reaches.

Now, in ECK you'll find there is a similarity of experiences. Why? Because of the principle As above, so below. First came the ECK, and then came the lower worlds. First came the ECK Masters and the ECK cosmology, and then came the creation below, the Kal creation, and the Lords of Karma.

When the doctor talks about masters who wear dark blue and purple colors, he's speaking of the masters of the Kal line versus the ECK line. These are the Lords of Karma and the administrators who work in that line.

Another interesting area he deals with is the debriefing that occurs after Soul leaves one life. You review your past life and reflect upon what you would like to do next time, what project you would like to undertake for your next lifetime.

Some people say, "I want to be in ECK so I never have to come back to earth again." People who need to come back will come back. Each Soul is taken to the level It belongs on. But if they're members of ECK, they do not come under the Lords of Karma. They come under the care of the Mahanta, the Living ECK Master. And under his care, the way is made

First came the ECK, and then came the lower worlds.

clear for you to have the greatest spiritual progress
that is possible.

There's also an area for people who have been
criminals. If a Soul is completely negative and has
hurt many others, that Soul is put into isolation for
a while to reflect. And if the guides for that particular Soul see that there is no hope for this Soul working
as It does, they remodel the Soul. They change the
atoms around. Once Soul is created, It's never destroyed, but Its atoms may be rearranged.

It's not done as a punishment. It's done to regen-
erate and allow this Soul to have the experiences
necessary to someday become a servant of God, a Coworker with God.

WHY DOES SOUL EXIST?

The good doctor tries to answer the question Why
do Souls exist? Why would God create imperfect Souls?
God creates Souls so that through their experiences,
It can know Itself in a greater way. It imparts to these
Souls the creative element of Itself, which is the Voice
of God, the ECK.

A part of this creative element is established in
each of you. So when you go through this life with
amnesia, trying to remember what your goal in this
life is, you have to put these creative powers to use.
Often what forces these creative powers into action
is hardship, problems, and roadblocks. Then it's up
to you as Soul, a spark of God, to exercise this God-
given creative power to figure a way out of the problem.

This is why Soul was created. God created Soul
simply so that God could know Itself better.

This book also goes into the actual process of
rebirth. When Soul comes back into a body, it's

God creates Souls so that through their experiences, It can know Itself in a greater way.

supposedly more traumatic than death. When I was young, many times I would have inner experiences of being born. It was claustrophobic and fearful.

AWAITING BIRTH

The doctor doesn't quite understand when Soul comes into the body. What does Soul do while the fetus is awaiting birth? Sometimes It flits around, moves in and out to check on the fetus.

The fetus is composed of a physical body, emotions, and mind. It's like a notebook computer that has its own functioning battery, and it looks like it's alive. But until somebody sits down at the keyboard and starts working with it, the computer is not going to be doing much work on its own. Well, that somebody who's going to do the work is Soul.

Soul establishes Itself in the physical body at first breath.

Soul establishes Itself in the physical body at first breath. This is the ECK teachings. And my feeling on abortion is this: when a fetus is at that stage where if it were born prematurely it could breathe on its own, it should then be allowed to breathe on its own.

When an infant dies, this has been agreed upon before by the parents and infant as Souls. A Soul agrees to come into the body for only a brief time. Sometimes these are filler lives. The infant comes for the benefit of the parents so they can learn some positive spiritual lesson like gratitude.

You'll find this book, *Journey of Souls,* very illuminating. And in a sense, Dr. Michael Newton is a servant of God.

I try to bring spiritual truth to you and give you the best, clearest teachings possible on the path of ECK. I want to let you know that all my love is with you on your journey home, both in this world and in the other worlds. May the blessings be.

ECK Springtime Seminar, San Francisco, California, Sunday, April 7, 1996

We take God's love for granted because it's as commonplace as the grass, the trees, the birds.

8
GOD'S LOVE
IN ACTION

od's love is around us all the time, so much so that most people are unaware of it. We take God's love for granted because it's as commonplace as the grass, the trees, the birds. It's so commonplace that we overlook it, even forget about it.

God's love flows equally to all people. But all people do not recognize God's love equally, because everyone's state of consciousness is different.

God's love flows equally to all people.

THE GIFT OF AWARENESS

We're all different. Some people are very aware and grateful for the blessings of God. Others just plod along through life saying, "Well, it's just life. What does God have to do with it?" So when we look at God's love in action, we're not talking about God's love in action as if it suddenly exists whereas before it never did. We're talking about our state of consciousness, recognizing this love of God that is with us all the time. Awareness—this is a hard thing.

For the last few years I've been ill, and I'm slowly regaining my health. It's taking a long time, but I'm working at it. Four years before I got really ill was the last time I went shopping for clothing. So the cuffs on my trousers were now totally worn through; it was embarrassing going to the chiropractor who'd put me on the table and check the lengths of my legs to see which muscles were tight. He held my feet up and stood there, looking at my heels, and the cuffs were totally worn away. It was embarrassing.

So finally about two weeks ago, my wife and I went shopping.

While I was in the men's store, she went over by the customer service area to the watch department to have the batteries replaced in our watches. For two years, we haven't been doing very much shopping or errands, except for very basic necessities. Clothes were not really basic necessities.

I found a couple of shirts and some trousers. I wanted my wife's opinion because I don't shop very often and I don't look at myself once I put the clothes on, but she has to. I thought, *Maybe it'd be one of those gentle courtesies in a marriage to ask her if these clothes matched and if she could stand looking at them.*

So I went wandering off through the men's store, very aware that the store detectives and everybody were probably watching this guy who's wandering around looking as if he's lost. But it had been five years since I'd been at this store, and I'd lost my bearings because they'd moved things around.

When I reached the customer service area, which is right next to the men's department, my wife wasn't there. The woman behind the counter asked, "Can I help you?" I looked around rather blankly because I was expecting to find my wife there. "I'm looking for my wife," I said.

"What does she look like?" the woman asked.

I stood there, and I thought for a long time. I was wondering, *How do you talk about qualities? How do you say, "My wife's a very good person; you'd know her right away"?* I was thinking about all these different things as I stood there. The woman decided to help me out. She'd been married for a while too; she was about my age. She knew men.

So, trying to help me out, she said, "What color of clothes was she wearing?" Even though before we'd left home earlier, I had said to myself, very carefully, *Pay attention when your wife comes in the room. See what clothes she's wearing,* I drew a blank.

"The color of her clothes?" I said. "Sure, I know the color of her clothes." I stood there, and I said, "She came here to have new batteries put into some watches." The woman looked at me and nodded; she knew I didn't know the color of anything. "The watch department is in that room over there," she said, so I walked over to the doorway, and I saw my wife. I looked back at the woman at the counter, and she could see my wife. I pointed, as if I was saying, "See what color she's wearing." I couldn't really have described the color anyway.

When we got home, I asked her, "What was that color you were wearing?" I thought it was somewhere between purple and violet, but it also looked somewhat blue. And she said, "It was a light periwinkle blue." I said, "Oh yeah, of course."

But while we were still in the store, I asked her, "Does this match? Can you stand the colors?" And she said sweetly, "It's very nice." So there was only the question of how to get back to the men's department from where my wife was having the watches worked on. There was the door next to customer service, which I did not want to go past, because the woman

I was wondering, How do you talk about qualities? How do you say, "My wife's a very good person; you'd know her right away"?

there was waiting, just looking at me, wanting to say, "Hmm, you found your wife? And the color of her dress, you knew it all along, didn't you?" Of course, I didn't want to lie, but I might have.

So I saw there was a side door which got rather close to the outside door of the store. I was carrying my new clothes, taking a real chance with the store detectives, going out this side door. But I said, "I'm going to do it." And I did. I got safely back into the men's department, I was able to pay for my clothing, and we finally left the store.

What a rare thing awareness is. We can be aware of all the great things in life, but if it gets down to my wife's clothing, I don't know what color she put on today.

God's Everyday Blessings

It's like this, too, with God's love. It is so commonplace we take it for granted, even though when we get up in the morning, we say, "I'm going to be aware of all God's blessings today." But we don't get more than five minutes into our day before we've already overlooked at least two, three, four blessings of the most obvious kind.

These blessings of God become more real to us because now we are aware of them.

What about the fact of being able to breathe and walk and think? To be able to move your hand when your mind says, "Pick up the spoon, and start eating the cereal"? We take all these little blessings for granted. Until there comes a time in our life when we lose the ability to do some of these things. And then, all of a sudden, life becomes very dear.

These blessings of God become more real to us because now we are aware of them. And how did we become aware of them? Usually through some hardship.

I'm not here to say that hardship is good. If I see hardship ahead, I usually try to go off to the left or to the right. I try to work my way around the hardship, because it makes good sense. But such is life. We move ahead, we do the best we can, and experience comes from not knowing any better.

We do something, and after we know better, then we don't do that again. This is called wisdom.

TWO-WAY FLOW

Divine love is a two-way thing. It flows to us from God, and when it comes to us, we as Soul must also give it back in some way to someone else. This is the nature of life. It flows. There is a two-way flow to everything.

President Kennedy said, "Ask not what your country can do for you; ask what you can do for your country." This was an amazing statement in the early 1960s, because it was pointing out to people that there is a better, fuller existence than simply taking from life. This fuller existence is giving something back to life. It's a change of consciousness.

As long as we want to get everything out of everyone and everything around us that we can without paying the full price, we're cheating ourselves. We're not living in accordance with the spirit of life. Because the spirit of life is a give-and-take proposition. Love flows in from God; Soul will eventually learn that Its love must flow back to God.

At the ECK Springtime Seminar in San Francisco, after the Sunday morning session, a woman named Michelle was standing in the bookroom with a lot of other people. She was going to take home some of the ECK materials. The long, zigzag line ran around the bookroom.

We do something, and after we know better, then we don't do that again. This is called wisdom.

Michelle noticed a mother and her daughter standing in line opposite her. The daughter was about four or five. The little girl had on a white dress and white ribbons in her hair.

Michelle looked at the little girl and said, "How pretty you are!" The little girl was embarrassed. She'd been a little bit bored just before this, because children have a hard time waiting in long lines. But she said politely, "Thank you."

Then the zigzag line moved along. Maybe ten minutes later, Michelle found herself standing in exactly the same place that the little girl had been standing. In line where she had been was a middle-aged man. He looked at Michelle and said, "I love your socks." She had loud, colored socks on. They really stood out.

Now Michelle was a little embarrassed, but she was polite. "Why, thank you," she said. "They're a lot of fun to wear."

This is an example of giving and receiving some of God's love. The love comes in, and you have to do something with it.

As she was standing there, she realized that the roles had been reversed: she had complimented the little girl, and the little girl had said thank you. It was love flowing from Michelle to someone else. Then as the line moved along, Michelle found herself in the little girl's spot, and the man standing in what had been Michelle's spot sends this very nice compliment to her. And she returned it, just as the little girl had.

This is an example of giving and receiving some of God's love. The love comes in, and you have to do something with it.

What made it good here is that not only was it about giving love, but it was also something fixed in time and space. The man took the place of Michelle, and Michelle took the place of the little girl.

Michelle was watching the crowd in the bookroom,

and she said, "Really, it's only about observing, and it's about consciousness." She was realizing that this is all that life is about. It's about observing and consciousness, being aware of what takes place around us.

HUNT FOR CURRY POWDER

Three friends, two women and a man, were at the ECK Springtime Seminar in San Francisco, and on Sunday afternoon they decided to go shopping. They went to Fisherman's Wharf and the other tourist places; then they caught a cab to go back to the hotel. While they were in the cab, it just came to one of the women: she would like to buy some good curry powder to use in cooking when she got home.

So they asked the cabdriver if he knew where there was a store that sold good curry powder. "Sure," he said. He was from Vietnam; he had been one of the boat people. He'd been in prison, escaped, and come to the United States fifteen years earlier.

As they were driving, the cabbie began talking about all the different recipes that he used curry powder in. They were just enjoying themselves, the four in the cab. They came to the first store, and the two women ran inside. No curry powder. This puzzled the cabdriver. He was not taking the ECKists for a ride, as some of you may suspect. This cabbie was honest. So he said, "I know of another store." They said, "OK." It was still on the way back to the hotel. No curry powder. Third place. No curry powder.

So the three friends asked him, "Is there any place you can recommend—even if it isn't on the way to the hotel?"

The driver knew a store that definitely had curry powder, but it would cost them a couple of dollars

She was realizing that this is all that life is about. It's about observing and consciousness, being aware of what takes place around us.

more. They said that was fine.

So when they got to the fourth place, the two women ran inside. The cabbie was quiet for a while, then he asked the man, "Are you married to one of the women?" The man said no, they were just three good friends. And the cabbie asked, "Where are you from?" The man said, "I'm from Canada." And he asked, "Where are the two women from?" The ECKist said, "One's from Canada; the other's from Mexico." It was real quiet for a while as the cabdriver was thinking about this. Finally he asked the man, "What are you in San Francisco for?" The man said, "We're here for Eckankar, Religion of the Light and Sound. There is a seminar here, and we're here to sing HU, which is a love song to God."

Then the man asked, "Would you like me to sing HU for you?"

Then the man asked, "Would you like me to sing HU for you?"

The cabdriver said, "Sure."

The ECKist sang HU one time. When he sang it the second and third time, the cabdriver joined in. They were sitting there, the two of them, singing HU, as the two women came back from the store with their precious little bag of curry powder.

The man told the two women that they'd been talking about Eckankar. So while they drove back to the hotel, the women talked about Eckankar to the driver and answered his questions. The man just sat there and observed what was happening.

San Francisco has some tremendously steep hills. I used to drive those hills, and I loved it. But you worry about your brakes because some of these hills go straight down. First of all, you've got to get to the top of the hill; you hope your car has got enough horsepower to make it. I had a very old car in those days, and sometimes it wouldn't make it to the top.

Once the car got to the top, the brakes had to be good enough to stop in time on the way down. I was always looking for a friendly tree to run up against.

So they started down this very, very steep hill. The cabdriver was very comfortable with San Francisco hills since he'd been there fifteen years. They got almost to the bottom, and the light was red. The cabbie stopped the taxi, shut his eyes, and took his hands off the wheel. He began to sing, "HU-U-U-U-U."

His passengers trust the Mahanta, the Inner Master, a lot, but this was a little bit more than they were ready for. So very quickly they suggested that while he was driving in traffic, especially with them in the car, that he not chant HU, especially with his eyes shut. A better place to do this would be at home after work.

The cabdriver agreed. He said he'd do it later. So they relaxed, and the talk turned back to a more balanced conversation again, between cooking and the ECK teachings. And so they got back to the hotel.

But when they got back, the man was thinking about how Divine Spirit, the ECK, had used this quest for curry powder to give the cabbie a chance to hear about HU, the love song to God. What made the cabdriver more comfortable was that all the people in his cab were from another country, even as he himself was new to the United States. He felt more receptive to hearing about HU from them than he would have been from someone born in the U.S. It was as if he were among friends. So it was very easy for him to hear about HU.

Divine Spirit, the ECK, had used this quest for curry powder to give the cabbie a chance to hear about HU, the love song to God.

SPECIAL MEAL

My problem with electromagnetic radiation has been severe. I try to stay away from anything that

generates it: the TV, computer, even electric fans.
There are two kinds of electromagnetic radiation—
from AC, or alternating current, and from DC, direct
current. I'm most sensitive to the radiation from
alternating current. Cars and planes generate mostly
direct current, and I can tolerate that radiation a
little better with certain electronic devices to help.
So my wife and I were able to fly to a seminar this
spring for the first time in two years.

On the plane, sitting by the window next to me,
was a little boy of seven. It was Easter weekend. It
looked like he was a child in a divorced family, with
one of his parents living in California, the other
parent in Minnesota.

The boy was flying on his own. He was very well
behaved, real quiet. He put his bag underneath the
seat in front of him, sat down very quietly, pulled out
a Garfield comic, and sat reading it. I tried not to
read over his shoulder too much. Garfield is one of
my favorite cartoon characters.

When he finished reading that comic, he picked
out a book and started reading that. I was thinking,
This little guy sure likes to read. It was all words, no
pictures. And this boy was only about seven.

One of his parents, whoever had sent him from
San Francisco to Minneapolis, had arranged a special meal for him, something he liked. When the
attendant said, "Anyone who has a special meal,
please press the call button," the little boy nudged
me. "Could you press the button for me?" So I did,
and a minute later the flight attendant came up.

I said, "This young man has a special meal." The
flight attendant asked the boy's last name, and the
boy said, "O'Brien." The flight attendant went away,
came back with a meal, and set it down.

My wife and I carried our own meal, basically bread and water because I can't handle any fats at this time. My wife has come up with a recipe for bread without any fat in it. And we carried our own water. So we're having bread and water, and when I looked over at the boy's meal, I saw pita bread with grated carrots inside. I said, "This poor guy is really in bad shape."

The little guy looked at his food very sadly and pushed it all the way back to the edge of his tray table. He just sat there and looked as sad as anyone I've ever seen. *Apparently it's not what he was expecting,* I thought. It didn't take a wizard to figure that out.

So I asked him, "Your mother asked them to give you this?" He said, "No." I said, "What were you expecting?" He said, "A hot dog." I said, "Well, that explains it." You're expecting a hot dog, and you get pita bread with grated carrots, a little bundle of grapes on the side, and some other suspect health foods.

I said, "I'll call the flight attendant for you if you like." He didn't say anything, so I did.

The flight attendant came over. I said, "He was expecting a hot dog." The flight attendant was very apologetic. He went away to find out what had happened.

Soon the flight attendant came back and told us there were two O'Briens on the flight and they had just given the wrong meal to the young gentleman. He said, "I'll get the other one right away." So he ran off.

They gave the little boy's pita bread with grated carrot to the other O'Brien, and the boy got his hot dog.

When the boy had finished the hot dog, he started looking around. There were a few other things on his tray, some grapes and healthy foods. Without touching anything but the wrappers, he took this food, bent over, and put it into his bag. In his world, there were hot dogs, and then there were health foods. He'd gotten rid of the big tray of health foods, but the hot dog had other health foods with it — a couple of grapes and other things he didn't particularly care for. The flight attendants were coming around to pick up trays, and when they were a couple of rows away, I said to the little boy, "Is there anything you'd like to get rid of?" Broad hint. He just looked at me and said, "No." He was perfectly satisfied with whatever happened to the food he stuck into his luggage.

So I let it be because I had to. There was nothing threatening his health. I realized that here, as with the other people in the earlier stories, I was just a person who was passing along God's love, helping a little boy get the food he wanted and had ordered. But he didn't want any help in getting rid of the food he wasn't eating. He had other plans for it. I had no idea what those were, and I wasn't going to ask.

These are the little things that go on every day. They happen to us, and we just take them for granted. We come home at night and tell our spouse, "A little thing happened on the plane." Sometimes it's so small a thing we even forget to mention it. It goes totally out of our minds, but it's God's love working through each and every one of us. It does it all the time.

> I was just a person who was passing along God's love, helping a little boy get the food he wanted and had ordered.

WAKING DREAM

An ECKist had a nice little pillow with a saying on it, "To err is human. To forgive, canine." It had a special meaning for her, because of a waking dream she had had.

The waking dream had followed an incident where

she had been very rude to her mother. This young woman hadn't been feeling very well, and her mother got into her line of fire. So the young woman had snapped at her. Later she wished she hadn't been so hasty and so angry.

After her mother had left, she wondered, *Should I make this right? Or should I just let it go and write it off as one of those little experiences in life? What should I do?* She didn't know.

She went in to take a shower. The question was still going through her mind. She took her shower and dried off, then she went to the sink to brush her teeth. All the time she was wondering, *Should I call my mom and apologize?* She took out her toothbrush, put some stuff on it, stuck it in her mouth, and started brushing.

Suddenly, she discovered she was brushing her teeth with soap.

She had meant to unscrew the top of the toothpaste and put it on her brush. Instead she had gone to the soap dispenser, which has a pump on it—a totally different mechanism—and squirted the soap on her toothbrush. Then she very calmly and placidly put the brush in her mouth and started cleaning her mouth out with soap.

Through this waking dream, she got the message from the Mahanta, the Inner Master. It was: clean up your act with your mother.

This little waking dream was God's love in action.

BECOMING MORE AWARE

These are all little examples of God's love in action, situations which happen all the time. The woman's experience with the soap made her more conscious about being hasty in her words to a loved one.

The woman's experience with the soap made her more conscious about being hasty in her words to a loved one.

I'm bringing out these examples because, once they're pointed out to you, most of you are going to pick up on them in your own lives. You're going to say, "I know something that happened to me just like that story. But it never occurred to me that something like this would be an example of God's love in action. I just never thought of it." We think God's love is something you get when you are praying before bedtime or in church on Sunday. We just never think it would be in stuff like brushing teeth with soap. But that's how it works.

Do You Use Creativity or Power?

A lot of people in an immature state of being like to control others, make them do this or that, usually saying it's for one good cause or another. They'll say, "This is a good cause, we're going to save our planet, and therefore we're going to do something with your property."

People in authority love to take away the property rights of other people in the name of some good cause.

People are always trying to control others under the guise of good intentions, whereas really they're breaking greater laws, having no respect for the rights of other people. People in authority love to take away the property rights of other people in the name of some good cause.

In their minds, the rights of other people give way to their particular cause, whatever it is. It's one of the signs of spiritual immaturity. This is not to say that we shouldn't take care of our homes and the cities and countries where we live, keep them clean and environmentally sound. But there's a way to do it without running roughshod over the rights of individuals.

If people in authority would use a little bit of their creative wisdom, they'd find other ways to reach this goal without having to use the strong arm of force. But of course, that is not their intention. They wish to use force, which is an example of none of God's love in action, I have to say.

LOVE HELPS US OVERCOME FEAR

An instructor at a university was putting together a curriculum. He taught graphic arts and computer design. He had the whole curriculum pretty well put together; he was an expert in the field. But the curriculum had to be approved by the provost, a high administration official.

The instructor felt that this provost had no scruples whatsoever. He liked to control people. He liked to make people jump through hoops because it gave him a sense of power.

The instructor was concerned that the provost was going to turn his curriculum upside down. This upset the instructor very much. So he went into contemplation to ask the Mahanta, the Inner Master, to give him an insight into this matter. What could he do? How should he regard this situation so that he could stay in balance?

What could he do? How should he regard this situation so that he could stay in balance?

He fell asleep during his contemplation and had a dream where he was at home in the kitchen with his wife. They were preparing a meal.

Suddenly in the dream a mad dog ran against the glass kitchen door, lunging at it. The glass was strong enough to keep the dog out. But the man began wondering in his dream, *What am I going to do about that dog?* In his hand, he was holding a wooden spoon. He thought, *I could try to drive the dog off with this wooden spoon.*

Then suddenly he stopped. *What am I doing? The dog can't get in. The dog's out there; I'm in here. Let*

*the dog stay out there, and I'll stay inside where it's
safe.*

When the man woke up, he realized what the
Inner Master, the Dream Master, was telling him:
As long as you stay within your state of consciousness, which is the secure place within your heart, no
outer fear or force can harm you.

As soon as he realized this, the man knew he had
his answer about the provost and the curriculum: Let
it be.

He realized that, as long as fear did not come into
his state of consciousness, no outside force of any
sort, not even a threat by his provost, could hurt him.

The gift of the Mahanta was to remind him of
God's love. Love always overcomes fear. And this is
what he learned through the dream. As soon as he
had this understanding, the provost no longer had
any power over him.

*The gift of the
Mahanta was
to remind him
of God's love.*

BLESSINGS OF GOD

An ECKist in Nigeria was traveling in a minibus.
He was scheduled to speak at an ECK regional seminar, give several talks, and also conduct several
workshops. As the bus was traveling along the highway in Nigeria, this man fell into what he called a
profound sleep. He slept for four hours and twenty
minutes.

Suddenly he was awakened by a loud noise. He
looked around, and everything was upside down.
People were standing outside the bus with axes trying to break through the windshield. He was seated
in the front row.

As he looked around, he noticed that some of the
people in the front row looked as if they'd gone through
a terrible ordeal. So he asked the man beside him,

"What happened?" He said, "While you were asleep, our minibus ran head-on into a water truck." The passengers were trapped inside the bus, and the people with the axes were trying to rescue them. But so far there was no danger to speak of, no fire, no lives lost. The other people seated in the front row all had broken limbs. But the ECKist was totally unharmed.

When the rescuers got the passengers off the bus, they looked at it. There should have been a lot of people hurt during this accident.

The next day, the ECKist continued his journey. He arrived at the ECK seminar safe and sound. He was very grateful for the blessings of God that had probably saved his life.

Sometimes these blessings—for no accountable reason that we can see—save people from a very serious fate.

There comes a time that all things pass on, and that happens to anyone, ECKist, Christian, or Buddhist. But at certain times in life, there are turning points. And it's a turning point whether a Soul could leave at that time through an accident or not. Sometimes the blessings of God come through the Mahanta, or through whatever avenue, to prolong the life of an individual. He or she has been making good spiritual progress, and this life is worth the experience. So the individual is allowed to go on for some years more. That is also God's love in action.

Sometimes the blessings of God come through the Mahanta, or through whatever avenue, to prolong the life of an individual.

A RETURN ON LOVE

One Friday afternoon, a woman named Phyllis was returning some clothes to a store. At the return desk, she began talking with the salesclerk, a very friendly woman in a bright new dress. While they were talking, other employees came up and constantly interrupted them. So Phyllis's clothing returns, which should only have taken a few minutes, took a long time. But Phyllis decided to be very patient and keep her sense of humor about the whole thing.

After she had returned the clothes, she spent the rest of the afternoon shopping.

Toward the middle of the afternoon, she suddenly had an awful feeling. She noticed a funny sensation in her mouth. *Uh oh,* she thought, *my tooth's chipped. That means the filling could fall out.* Here it was, Friday afternoon, right before the weekend. It looked like she was facing a long weekend of discomfort unless she could get to her dentist before he closed the office.

Many of you have had this experience. Right before a long weekend, something goes wrong with a tooth or you suddenly have to go to a doctor. Everything's closed, and somehow you go through this entirely miserable weekend wondering, *Why do these things always happen to me?*

When Phyllis arrived at her dentist's office, she found the door locked. She stood outside, holding her jaw with one hand, wondering what she's going to do for the whole weekend with this chip out of her tooth.

A stream of water was pouring out from between the ceiling tiles. Evidently some plumbing had broken.

As she was standing there, she happened to look down at the rug in the lobby and saw that it was soaked with water. In fact, there was a big puddle of water right in front of her. So her eyes traveled up the wall to the ceiling. A stream of water was pouring out from between the ceiling tiles. Evidently some plumbing had broken. So even though she had her own problem, her dentist had a bigger one.

Phyllis looked around to see if there was someone she could tell about this water leak. She saw a lit doorway. She walked toward it, knocked, and went in. She found a receptionist sitting at a desk.

Phyllis said, "A water pipe has sprung a leak out in the hall. I just thought you'd like to know about it so that you could find someone to fix it before the weekend."

The receptionist thanked her very kindly and then said, "Now, what can I do for you?"

This took Phyllis by surprise. She said, "I have this chipped tooth but my dentist is already gone for the weekend."

The receptionist said, "The dentist I work for is still here. Just a minute." She left the room.

A few minutes later she came back and said, "Can you come back in an hour? The doctor will be able to see you then." Phyllis said, "Sure." Phyllis came back in an hour, and the dentist very efficiently and cheerfully put a temporary filling in her tooth. When he finished, she shook his hand very gratefully and said, "What do I owe you?"

He said, "No charge, that's what I'm here for."

When you hear a story like this, you think, *This must have happened on some other planet.* But it was earth, one of those wonderful little corners of earth that's still a better time and a better place.

Without making a big thing about it, maybe God's love in action had now come to bestow its blessings upon her.

Phyllis realized that because she had tried to be pleasant to other people in very unpleasant circumstances, without making a big thing about it, maybe God's love in action had now come to bestow its blessings upon her.

STRENGTHENING A MARRIAGE

One day I went to a grocery store, and an ECKist was working there. I'll call him Jim.

Jim was unpacking vegetables and fruits. As he

He asked,
"What are
some ways to
strengthen a
marriage?"

was stocking the shelves, I was shopping. As we both worked in our separate ways, we talked. He asked, "What are some ways to strengthen a marriage?"

So while I looked through the potatoes, I tried to think of a good answer for ways to strengthen a marriage. I said, "Learn to forgive and forget the small slights that take place in every relationship."

And I said, "Don't press each other's buttons." An argument usually starts in a family because the two people know each other so well, and they know exactly how to get their mate upset. So when there's an argument, they talk about exactly those things. They figure that's what an argument is for.

The third thing I mentioned was, "Practice silence on days when your mate is having a bad-hair day." I had finished my answer, so Jim went his way in the store, and I went my way.

Then I turned the corner, and I heard this big, booming voice. It was Jim's supervisor. He was a very stocky man, built like a rock. He was wearing a T-shirt that said, "Center of the electromagnetic universe." He looked as if he could have been the center—very strong.

He was writing on a clipboard. Apparently, he was working with Jim, seeing which fruits and vegetables were in low supply and needed to be reordered. Then he made a mistake. He took his pencil and started erasing furiously on his pad. Then he said, "The best, most useful invention of mankind—the eraser!"

And I thought, *There is the ECK, Divine Spirit, giving the Golden-tongued Wisdom to Jim about his question, How do you strengthen a marriage?*

The supervisor gave Jim a down-to-earth answer: The best, most useful invention of mankind—

the eraser! If you make a mistake, erase it. If someone else makes a mistake, erase it from your memory. This was the Golden-tongued Wisdom, an aspect of the ECK-Vidya, the ancient science of prophecy, speaking to Jim very directly.

I wanted to run up to Jim and say, "Did you get it? Did you hear it?"

I don't know if he heard it, because just then another person asked him a question about the produce.

A few minutes later my wife and I finished shopping, and we left. I said, "I wonder if Jim got it. Did he see this demonstration of God's love in action?"

Jim had asked me a question, and I gave him a threefold answer that was a little hard to remember. But Divine Spirit, speaking through his supervisor, said it very simply: "The best, most useful invention of mankind—the eraser!"

That's probably the best way to strengthen a marriage—use the eraser. Don't press buttons. Some days, if your mate is feeling off, erase it from your memory. Just erase it, if you love each other.

God's love in action—look for it everywhere because it is all around you, all the time. It is God's love flowing to you. And when Soul becomes aware, It finds that It must always return this love to the divine source from which it came.

You are Soul. Learn your purpose in life, which is to become a vehicle for this divine love.

Divine Spirit, speaking through his supervisor, said it very simply: "The best, most useful invention of mankind— the eraser!"

ECK Summer Festival, Saturday, June 15, 1996, Montreal, Quebec, Canada

Divine Spirit, the Holy Spirit, watches out for each of you, for your safety and spiritual well-being, with as much care as a llama looks after the sheep in its care.

9

IN THE GRASP
OF DIVINE LOVE

I was talking to a friend this morning. We were discussing llamas. Llamas are from South America; they're long-necked, beautiful animals. I'd heard that llamas make excellent sheepdogs, that they watch sheep better than sheepdogs. So I asked about it.

He and his wife own a farm in the eastern part of the United States. They have llamas and sheep, and outside the fence they have coyotes.

The coyotes spend their time trying to figure out if it's worth it to go inside the fence to get the sheep. But inside the fence is also where the llamas are. I asked him, "Are llamas really that good at protecting sheep?" He said, "Yes, they're very protective of sheep." Sometimes a coyote comes inside the fence and gets chased off by a llama. So the coyote goes someplace else that is less interesting.

A llama has a peculiar warning cry. It sounds like a siren. The first time our friend heard this siren sound, he had no idea what was going on. He ran outside, prepared for just about anything, and there was the llama sending a warning to a coyote or some other animal that was thinking about coming into the flock of sheep.

How does this fit into the title, "In the Grasp of Divine Love"? You have to consider that Divine Spirit, the Holy Spirit, watches out for each of you, for your safety and spiritual well-being, with as much care as a llama looks after the sheep in its care. Llamas are interesting, and the Holy Spirit is interesting too.

WHAT IS THE HOLY SPIRIT?

God's Voice at Its highest and most basic level is the Light and Sound.

I studied religion for many years as a Lutheran, and the Holy Spirit was always an indefinable thing to me. I could never quite get a handle on It. The Holy Spirit wasn't quite a person, yet It was a person, part of the Trinity. Its aspects were very hard for me to understand. But coming into Eckankar years ago, I learned that the Holy Spirit, or the ECK, is the twin action of God's Voice. God's Voice at Its highest and most basic level is the Light and Sound.

Everything exists in this world and every other world because of the Light and Sound. Even the absence of light depends upon light so that there can be an absence of it, if you will. Everything in all creation depends upon the Light and Sound for its existence.

There is a wave which comes from God. It is the Voice of God, the Sound Current, made up of both the Light and the Sound. It speaks to us in different ways, sometimes through intuition, sometimes through a messenger speaking for the spiritual hierarchy, like a guardian angel. Sometimes people hear a voice. They'll say, "God spoke to me," or "The Holy Spirit spoke to me," but it was actually a guardian angel, one of the many workers in the spiritual realm. They are all working with God, at a certain level.

The Holy Spirit also speaks to us through dreams. Many people, at least in my old religion, didn't have much use for dreams except as they happened in the Bible years ago. For instance, Joseph of the Old Testament had many dreams.

The prophets had dreams. They used dreams to give moral direction to the nation or to a group of people. Dreams are a very important way for the Holy Spirit to speak to people.

SPIRIT TOUCHES EVERYONE

The Holy Spirit touches a person's heart regardless of the religion the individual happens to belong to. The Holy Spirit doesn't care whether you are Catholic or Greek Orthodox or Protestant or Hindu or Muslim. The Holy Spirit doesn't care.

The Holy Spirit touches a person's heart regardless of the religion the individual happens to belong to.

This is one of the universal aspects of the Holy Spirit that people in their various religions have overlooked. Almost every religion acts as if they have a particular claim to God and the Holy Spirit. It's funny, if you stop to think about it. People say, "We have the best understanding of who God is and how it all works." Then it extends a little bit further until they say, "Our understanding is right, and everybody else's understanding is wrong."

Be that as it may, it may or may not be true as far as things can be true on earth, this being an imperfect world. That's a human being's opinion about God and Holy Spirit. But what about the opinion of God and the Holy Spirit about this particular point of view? In other words, does God favor the Catholics over the Methodists or the people of the Episcopal church? Or doesn't God care? Or doesn't the Holy Spirit care either?

God and the Holy Spirit don't divide the world up

into a number of different religions and denominations the way we do. That's why the Holy Spirit can and will touch people, regardless of their religion.

This is why there are very pious people in every faith. I'm speaking of truly pious people, not those who put on a Sabbath-day or Sunday act for their neighbors. Truly pious people are found in every religion, in every faith. You also have a lot of people who are just average in any religion. And then you have some people where you wonder, *How can they even claim to belong to any religion?* Because they treat their fellow beings so poorly; because they use God as an excuse to harm other people. Those people may claim to be in a religion, but they don't belong in any religion.

Why are some people more saintly and others less saintly? Perhaps it's because of the maturity or immaturity of a particular Soul.

How does this happen? Did God create some people more spiritually evolved than others? Or is there more to it? Reincarnation and karma play a very strong role in the spiritual unfoldment of each individual, of each person, of you.

Reincarnation and karma play a very strong role in the spiritual unfoldment of each individual, of each person, of you.

GATES OF LIFE AND DEATH

A woman spent twelve years of her life in business, becoming very successful. She went after one goal, then another. She felt a need to belong to one of the big-name companies, and she wanted an important title in one of these companies. This was her goal. She pursued it for twelve years.

Five years ago, she had an organ transplant which took her right to the gates of life and death. She recovered from the operation very nicely, but it was an awakening for her. And she began to wonder.

The woman began to ask, "What am I here for?" She looked her life over and said, "Basically I've been here to serve myself all this time." She realized that during the years she had spent in the corporate world, she had been serving the ego, her smaller self, the little self. She had learned a lot about corporate ways, she had learned a lot about other people. But more importantly, she had learned a lot about herself.

The organ transplant was a wake-up call. Very gradually it came to her that there must be another purpose to life.

LOVE REPLACING FEAR

These changes don't always arrive one day as a clear awakening, where the person says, "The Lord spoke to me and said, 'You're going to be my missionary now'" or something like this. It happens gradually. Over the past five years, she came to the realization that her purpose in life was to serve life with love. She looked back over different things she'd done — she's an artist too — and she realized that the love had gone out of her art. *When and why did this happen?* she wondered. As she was working in the corporate world, she'd noticed, as the years went on, that she had more and more fear. She'd lost the love and gained the fear. "What went wrong these last twelve years?" she asked.

One day several months ago, she was having an important meeting with her boss, and suddenly it seemed to her that this meeting was a turning point. Something wasn't going right in the meeting. It was almost as if her boss was setting her up to take responsibility for things that weren't really her responsibility. This would put her on the firing line in the future. A feeling was building inside her: It was

The organ transplant was a wake-up call. Very gradually it came to her that there must be another purpose to life.

The Voice of God sometimes speaks through guardian angels, dreams, intuition, and the Mahanta also, who in ECK we speak of as the Inner Master.

time to leave. But she couldn't find a good reason.

Suddenly, the Inner Master, the Mahanta, gave her a very strong impression that said, "Leave today." So the woman gave notice that very day.

God always speaks through the Holy Spirit because It's the Voice, the Word, of God. The Holy Spirit, the ECK, is the Word of God. The Voice of God sometimes speaks through guardian angels, dreams, intuition, and the Mahanta also, who in ECK we speak of as the Inner Master. So the Mahanta said to her, "Leave today." And she did; she just left.

Not long after she left the corporate race of twelve years, she looked back over her life and asked herself, "What has changed in my life since the operation five years ago?" She remembered that about a year ago she had had this strong inner nudge to begin doing volunteer work of some kind because her life felt so unfulfilled. The love had gone, and fear had come in to take its place. So she took an extensive training course at the same university hospital where she'd had the organ transplant and became one of the people who gave attention to babies who are born prematurely, preemies.

My daughter was born prematurely; she was just over three pounds at the time. She was in the children's hospital where we lived in California, and my wife was in another hospital. I'd commute between the children's hospital, my wife's hospital, and work. It was a very busy time—for months. My daughter was this little bitty baby in the incubator. I would put my hand in there every day, just to let her hold my little finger. My little finger isn't big, but she was very small. I could hold her in the palm of my hand. She draped over the edges, but she was tiny.

So this businesswoman became a preemie cuddler.

Some of these preemies weren't big, the way my daughter was at three pounds. Some of these weighed only one pound. It's hard to imagine how small a baby would be at one pound.

As the woman looked into the eyes of these babies, there was never any fear. She saw agelessness, love, and wisdom, but never fear. Even when the nurses came in to siphon the ventilators and their mouths and their throats so that they could breathe, so that they could grow larger and finally take care of breathing by themselves, there was never any fear. It might have been anger because these little people were very upset that anyone would treat them in such an uncivilized way. If they were crying, it wasn't because they were afraid. They were just a little bit angry at the indignity of it all.

As the woman looked into the eyes of these babies, there was never any fear. She saw agelessness, love, and wisdom, but never fear.

FAITH BEING TESTED

My daughter cried and made an awful racket. I often used to kid her later, "There were babies in there who cried, but there was one that sounded like a crow. That was you." And she did. My daughter could really raise a racket, and it was embarrassing. Her face would turn very red, and she'd just scream.

Then of course she grew bigger and bigger, and gradually she graduated from the incubator, from grade school, and from high school, thank goodness. For those of you who have young children, remember that there is light at the end of the tunnel.

As your children go through the teen years you wonder, *Am I really in the grasp of divine love? Who would have given you this child?*

During the teen years we find such strange energies coming through us, feelings of rebellion and wanting to fly out of the nest, but afraid because the nest is seven feet up in the tree. Yet you have this urge to fly from the nest.

This is what the youth are fighting, and this is what most of us fought when we were teenagers. Sometimes we were unkind to our parents or even ashamed of them.

It's at this point the parents ask, "Are we really in the grasp of divine love?" It tests your faith to have a teenager, and it tests your faith to be a teenager.

In the Grasp of Divine Love

One day this businesswoman did a spiritual exercise and met one of the ECK Masters, Fubbi Quantz, at the Katsupari Monastery. The Katsupari Monastery is located on the physical plane, but it's not a place that people can see with their physical eyes. It's a real place, but it's very well protected.

Fubbi Quantz took her into a room for healing.

It's a round room. Some of you may have been there. The room is domed. What look like slats go up into the ceiling. If you've ever been inside a silo with a steel roof, you may know what I'm talking about; that's the closest I can come to describing it. But it's a large room, larger than the top of a silo.

After the Light and Sound of God had come to her, she felt stronger.

There is a cot. It looks as if it might be a hard cot, but it's very comfortable. It's a healing place. You just go there and rest. The Light and Sound currents are used to bathe the person who has come for healing.

After the Light and Sound of God had come to her, she felt stronger. She began wondering about the future course of her life. Fubbi Quantz said, "The ECK has you firmly in the grasp of divine love. So, no need to worry. A perfect design is woven, and you are a strand in it. Be quiet and purposeful in this phase of your life."

This was the answer she needed. She got it through the spiritual exercise.

WHAT IS TRUE PRAYER?

Spiritual exercises are the way to become more aware of this life. Spiritual exercises, contemplation, and prayer of the right kind are all the same. Basically, it's opening your heart to God or the Holy Spirit and listening.

Correct prayer is listening to God.

Correct prayer is listening to God. If a person is going to err in prayer, it's through too much telling or talking to God. There's nothing wrong with telling or asking; there's nothing wrong with talking to God. But after you've asked your question, listen. Be quiet and listen.

Listening is true prayer, prayer of the highest sort. Even prayer where you're asking God something is of a high sort, or it can be. But sometimes people carry it to extremes.

When I was a child, my parents had us say our childhood prayers at bedtime. As I grew up and went to divinity school, I would still say my prayers at night. Not that those of us at divinity school were very righteous. A very small percentage were truly pious, and the rest of us were about average. We got along. We knew God was there. We did our lessons; we did our Bible study and science and math. There were also those in divinity school who were quite nonpious.

I used to say my prayers nightly, but away from home I could try out my wings a little bit. Some nights I'd just lie there and ask God for all kinds of things. I'd ask God for riches. I'd ask God to get rid of my toothaches. They came from all the sugar I ate; I hadn't made the connection between sugar and tooth decay. Every Sunday I'd go to the bakery and buy all this wonderful chocolate, all these jelly-filled rolls— I'd just stuff myself. I'd buy enough for my friends too. It took me years to figure out what I was doing, and I think the toothaches helped. Life has a way of teaching us better.

This is what I learned about prayer, that sometimes there is a wrong sort of prayer: you ask God to take away a toothache when basically you should stop eating the things that give you the toothache. But that's how we learn.

People ask God to make them rich, and at the same time they squander their money. They have done this their whole lives. What kind of a prayer is that? It's a prayer of irresponsibility. You're not taking responsibility for your own welfare. I'm not talking about people who through the circumstances of life find themselves in a bad situation or after being retired for twenty years find that inflation has eaten into their savings and it's very difficult for them to take care of themselves. These are very real problems. If these people ask God for help, you would expect that. But mostly, true prayer is listening to God.

HELP FROM GOD

Divine love is the Holy Spirit, God's love sent down to earth. This divine love works through the Light and Sound; it is Light and Sound. But taken together we just call it divine love.

Divine love is the Holy Spirit, God's love sent down to earth.

A husband and wife in their seventies were on vacation in California. He has a heart condition, so they carried oxygen. He had to be very careful not to get into strenuous situations.

As they were driving along the highway on a hot, windy California day, a back tire blew out. The husband guided the car over to the side of the road and got out. Both of them were wondering, *How are we going to fix the tire?* After a few minutes the wife said, "We'd better start fixing that tire because nobody's stopping to help us." The husband said, "Well, at the service station the lug nuts are put on with pneumatic wrenches. We're not going to get them off ourselves."

The wife didn't know what to do. She needed to clear her mind; she needed to sing HU. HU, this ancient love song to God, is a spiritual exercise or a prayer. As you sing HU, you're not asking God to help you. You're saying that whatever needs to be in life, you are willing to accept it, no matter what it is. In other words, you're simply saying, "Thy will be done." This is true prayer. Not my will, but Thy will be done. And singing HU is one of the ways to do a true prayer.

This is true prayer. Not my will, but Thy will be done. And singing HU is one of the ways to do a true prayer.

The woman went up the road to walk their springer spaniel, and she sang HU as she walked. This put her into the higher state, the Soul state. She felt calm and peaceful, full of trust. She came back and told her husband, "We're going to have to unload our luggage from the trunk, get at the jack, and start changing the tire ourselves."

No sooner had she said this than a battered old pickup truck pulled up right in front of them.

GUARDIAN ANGEL

The man who got out was a summertime Santa Claus. He was a big hefty man. The wind was blowing, and he had one button holding his shirt together at the top. His belly button was huge, and it was sticking out. They were in the area of central California where almonds grow, but the woman thought his navel was as big as a walnut. These are the little details that people notice when things go wrong on the road. A tire blows out and you're not well enough to take care of it yourself, so here comes your guardian angel sent by the Holy Spirit.

The man was very good natured. He came up to the couple and said, "What can I do to help you?"

They said, "Well, we need to change the tire."

He said, "I'm here to serve the Lord."

You see how the Holy Spirit works. She had sung HU, which was saying, "Not my will, but thine be done." Then, not understanding what to do next, she went back to the car to do something. You always try to do something. She told her husband that they would have to do the best they could. But before they could even start, the Holy Spirit sent someone to help them. And the first thing this person says is, "I'm here to serve the Lord."

The Holy Spirit sent someone to help them. And the first thing this person says is, "I'm here to serve the Lord."

The man helped the husband and wife unpack their luggage. Once they got to the jack, the man put it underneath the car, jacked it up, and changed the tire. He fixed everything and helped them put their luggage back in the trunk.

"Thank you very much," said the woman. "Can I pay you something?"

And the man said, "No charge; I'm a very wealthy man."

"You must be very strong," she said, "the way you broke those lug nuts loose from the wheel."

The man said, "I've had two bypass operations, and I'm not as strong as I used to be. Now, I'm just doing the Lord's work."

The man said, "My name is Harold." Suddenly

the woman noticed that his license plate was from Minnesota. And he was driving a blue truck.

LIGHT AND SOUND

In Eckankar blue is a very special color. Very often one of the manifestations of the Holy Spirit that people see is a blue light. This is one of the manifestations of the Holy Spirit. It's the Blue Light of the Mahanta, the Inner Master.

Sometimes people see a white light, yellow light, green light, pink light. Sometimes it's a very brilliant light; sometimes a very soft, subdued light. That's the Light, one part of the Holy Spirit, the Voice of God, the Word of God.

The other part is the Sound. There are many sounds that people may hear which show that the Holy Spirit is coming into their state of consciousness. Sometimes during prayer or contemplation, people will hear a buzzing like bees. Sometimes it might sound like a high electrical sound. Sometimes like a chorus of voices chanting a word, or a choir. Other times it may sound like birds singing in spring. Or the sound of a single musical instrument. There is a lot of variety in how these very high aspects of the Holy Spirit come to the individual, to you. These are all part of your spiritual education and spiritual enrichment.

Before he was Paul, Saul, on the road to Tarsus, saw the Light. It shone down very brightly. This was an aspect of the Holy Spirit.

There will often be a small voice that comes. This is the Voice of God. Maybe it's an angel speaking, but it's the action of the Voice of God. It can also be a sound like thunder or the sound of a jet plane high overhead. It can be anything.

Very often one of the manifestations of the Holy Spirit that people see is a blue light.

WHEN FEAR TAKES OVER

The man had said, "No charge; I'm a very wealthy man." So often people today—especially in our materialistic society—are looking for wealth. They're looking for wealth because they see it as a way to material freedom.

If you can own a home instead of renting, you won't have the landlord coming over all the time wanting to see if the place is OK. He'll use some excuse, "Oh, I have to check the plumbing today." But he's really coming in to look around and see how you are taking care of the property.

You're never quite secure in your own home as long as you rent. So you try to buy a home. It gives you more freedom of a material kind, where you don't have to wash the dishes, you don't have to worry about anyone coming in if you don't feel like it. You can decide, on a particular day, that you need to rest, that rest is more important than taking care of the dishes today.

When fear begins to take over, the love goes away, and that's your sign that you've gone too far.

This is why people want to accumulate wealth. They often want to make their lives more secure, better for their family or loved ones. It's a noble undertaking. But when it becomes the only goal in life, to the exclusion of everything else, fear begins to take over. The love goes away, and that's your sign that you've gone too far.

RECOGNIZING DIVINE LOVE

In Johannesburg, South Africa, there is an ECKist who is very good at computer programming. He was trying to put together an ECK program for a fair in his city, a program about the ECK teachings that would be interesting to people. One of the segments of it had portraits of certain ECK Masters, one after another, appearing on the screen.

The children loved his presentation. They'd watch all the animated Eckankar scenes and the ECK Masters on his monitor.

One young woman came walking by and stopped at the booth. She wanted to know, "Who's that Chinese Master there?"

And Douglas, the ECKist, said, "That's Lai Tsi."

"Every time I've come past your booth, this Master happens to be on the computer," she said. "He's been my guide here in my life, and I just wondered who he was. I didn't know his name." They got to talking about the ECK Master Lai Tsi.

Lai Tsi works pretty much on the inner planes with people who have been his students in past lifetimes to prepare them to come to the path of Eckankar today. So, without knowing it, this woman was in the grasp of divine love. She was drawn to see this special computer program that Douglas had put together just because he liked to work with computers and because he wanted to give people at the fair a fresh look at the teachings of ECK. It caught her attention.

She wanted to know, "Who's that Chinese Master there?" And Douglas, the ECKist, said, "That's Lai Tsi."

YOUR NEXT STEP

This woman has a choice whether or not to take another step on the path of ECK. Whether she does or not, the experience showed her something. It showed her that no one is ever left alone in this world. At some point, when it's time—whether it's the path of ECK or some other path—the Holy Spirit will lead you to the next step in your spiritual unfoldment.

It comes when you have grown spiritually, when you outgrow the nest in which you were born and raised. If you're a Catholic, you may become a Lutheran. If you're a Lutheran, you may become a

Methodist or you may join the Presbyterian Church. Or you may become a Hindu or a Buddhist.

This change may cause all sorts of problems in your family, because they don't understand why you came into their family in the first place. They don't understand that you are actually responding to the nudgings of the Holy Spirit because you have grown spiritually and are ready for the next step. Just because you visit an ECK seminar doesn't mean that you're ready for ECK, but it may mean you're ready for a change, perhaps even within your own religion. You may be ready to find the love that is in your religion.

Every religion comes from God. Every true religion that teaches the high principles of spiritual freedom and self-responsibility is of a divine nature.

So you may find what you need for the next step of your spiritual life in your own religion. Don't go running off to some other place just because you're bored or you think you don't have anything more to learn where you are. Look again.

You may be ready to find the love that is in your religion.

Life's Detour Signs

A young woman was taking off from work one day to go to an ECK seminar. She was afraid to drive alone because it was such a long distance to the seminar city and she wasn't used to driving long distances by herself. But she set off anyway.

After she had been driving for an hour, she stopped at a service station. There she met a family. The family made this particular drive many times each year. So when the family got back in their car, the young ECKist decided to follow them because it felt more comforting. She followed them all the way to the seminar, as if the other car was her guardian angel. She got to the seminar safely.

She was being very, very careful with her money because she had bills coming due. But when she was browsing in the seminar bookroom, she saw Mary Carroll Moore's book *Turning Points*. For some reason, she felt she just had to have it. So she bought it, even though she didn't know why.

After the seminar, as she was driving home, she saw something strange. Right outside of a town, in the middle of a big empty field was this hand-lettered sign: "Turn around."

She said, "That's strange, did I miss the turn? Is the Inner Master, the Mahanta, trying to tell me I missed the turn and I should turn around?"

Not long after that, she saw another sign, an orange construction sign that said, "Do not change lanes." So she took that as a sign from the Inner Master, from the Voice of God. Whatever that other sign had said, it didn't matter; this one said, "Don't change lanes." So she stayed in her lane. Every fifty feet or so for the next little while, there was one construction sign after another. These signs led her through the town. One would say, "Slow traffic"; another said, "Lane change ahead" or "Detour." Even though the route was new, she got through the town very nicely.

When she arrived home, she unpacked. And as she was unpacking, she came across the book *Turning Points*. So she opened it and looked inside.

Usually she doesn't pay any attention to the foreword, just passes over it quickly, but this time she began reading it. Mary Carroll Moore had written something to the effect that when we're ready for a change in life, life will put up signs to warn us that a change is coming. And this is exactly what the

She said, "That's strange, did I miss the turn? Is the Inner Master, the Mahanta, trying to tell me I missed the turn and I should turn around?"

woman needed at that point.

She sat down and began to read the book because she knew it was time for her to move forward spiritually. She found much help in it. The book came into her hands because she was in the grasp of divine love.

A Prophetic Dream

After this, she began trying to think of a way she could give back some of this divine love that she had received from God. Then she had a dream.

In the dream, she met a mother and daughter who had just moved to a new town. The daughter had started going to the high school there, but it was a very uncomfortable transition. At the new school, the other students looked at her as being different. In the dream the mother and daughter were about to turn around and walk away, when the daughter dropped a brochure. The ECKist picked it up to hand back to the young girl. She saw that it was an Eckankar brochure. As she handed the brochure back to the girl, she said, "So you're ECKists."

The mother and the daughter looked at the dreamer and said, "Yes, are you?"

"Yes," the dreamer told them.

"Do you know anyone else in town who are members of Eckankar?" the girl asked.

When the woman woke up, she said, "The name of that girl seems to be Jamie." She wrote it down in her notebook and forgot all about it.

A little while later, the local area was having an introductory talk on Eckankar at the library, and this young woman was going to give the talk. About six people had come. Just as she was about to begin, a girl walked in the door. She looked familiar, but her

She began trying to think of a way she could give back some of this divine love that she had received from God. Then she had a dream.

hair was dyed green. "Well, that's different," the ECKist said to herself.

During the talk, the girl asked all sorts of intelligent questions of a spiritual nature. She wanted to know about God. Her green hair was her sign of rebellion against her previous upbringing. She was crying out, but she didn't know how to deal with it.

When the talk was over, a car alarm suddenly went off in the parking lot. The woman recognized it as her own. So she ran outside, but there was no one there.

Just before she'd left home that day, she had decided to bring an ECK book, *Ask the Master,* Book 1, with her. She had put the book on the front seat of her car, and as she shut off her car alarm, she saw the book. So she took it inside and gave it to the girl with green hair. They exchanged names and the ECKist gave the girl her phone number.

Later, as the ECKist was home writing in her dream journal about all of the events of the day, she had a nudge to look back through the entries. She came across her dream of a few days before. And she noticed that in the dream, the girl's name was Jamie. It startled her because the girl who had looked familiar at the ECK talk had said her own name was Jamie. So this young girl is also in the grasp of divine love, as is the ECKist. The ECKist was giving back love, by giving an ECK introductory talk so that others could hear about the Sound and Light of God.

The ECKist was giving back love, by giving an ECK introductory talk so that others could hear about the Sound and Light of God.

LESSON ON MUSIC AND PHYSICS

A worker in the aerospace industry has played the guitar for eighteen years. He began having a series of dreams that showed him playing bass guitar, but he didn't know how to play bass. But the dreams kept coming, and so eventually he said, "I'm going to buy a bass guitar and take lessons so that I can become a very good bass player."

A while back, he had written a song that became popular among ECKists. But he had become attached to the song and hadn't written any others. He's learning and growing spiritually very nicely, but he realized that he was afraid to write any other songs, because maybe people wouldn't like the new songs as well as they had liked the previous song. He didn't know what to do.

The Golden-tongued Wisdom is actually another version of the Holy Spirit speaking to a person. Sometimes it speaks through another human being. And one day it happened to this ECKist.

His music teacher said, out of the blue, "If you write music, write it with love, and then play it with love. It doesn't matter what people think about it."

Suddenly this man realized that the technical expertise of writing and playing music is one thing, but unless you do it with love, you're doing it for nothing. If you're going to do something, do it with love so that it can help you and others spiritually.

Not long after, this ECKist had another dream. This time he was with an ECK Master, who was giving him a lesson in physics. In the dream, the man asked this ECK Master, "Would man ever travel faster than the speed of light?"

The ECK Master said, "We already do at night, in the Soul body."

Then the ECK Master went on. "The physical barrier of light cannot be penetrated by physical matter such as your body or even a spaceship. At the speed of light, matter changes states. Physical molecules are held together here by objects moving at

The Golden-tongued Wisdom is actually another version of the Holy Spirit speaking to a person.

the speed of light." Most of us, in this kind of conversation, would be shaking our heads by this time, asking, "What's this guy talking about?" The ECK Master saw that the ECKist had the most bewildered look on his face. The Master laughed and said, "The speed of light is the separation between the Physical Plane and the Astral Plane. Each of the planes, except beyond the Soul Plane, has a similar barrier. The Souls that live there see this barrier, and it is not until they step upon the path of ECK that they can see beyond it."

So this aerospace worker and musician got a lesson in physics. Some of this information might be handy for those of you who are working in the field of space travel and spiritual unfoldment.

The speed of light is the separation between the Physical Plane and the Astral Plane.

WHITE LIGHT OF GOD

A woman from Ghana was scheduled to have minor surgery on her hand. The doctor had been very considerate and said he'd try to fit her in earlier than she was scheduled because it was such a minor operation. Because he would use a general anesthetic, he told her, "Don't eat or drink anything before the operation."

The woman arrived at the clinic early that morning to be put on a list in case there was an opening in the doctor's schedule.

She had a problem with low blood sugar, and she could only go for twelve hours without food or drink or she would be in danger of collapse. She calculated when she arrived at the clinic that since she hadn't had any food or drink since midnight, she would only be good until about noon. But the hospital list said she was scheduled for 2:00 p.m. She didn't know what she'd do if the doctor didn't have room for her earlier.

Around 10:00 a.m., she wasn't feeling well, so the woman went into the nurse's office. The nurse happened to be a friend of hers she hadn't seen for years. The nurse let the woman rest in her office for several hours while she waited. As she rested, she remembered something her sister had told her. Her sister had said, "When it's going past your twelve hours, remember to sing HU." So the ECKist began singing HU. She fell asleep and had a dream.

In her dream, she had her right hand out, the hand that was going to have the operation. Someone was pouring warm tea into it. It felt very good. She wished it wouldn't stop.

Suddenly someone slammed the door very loudly. She opened her eyes, and she was looking right into her doctor's face.

He said, "I'm sorry to have to tell you this, but so many emergencies have been coming in all day I won't be able to get to you until 4:00 p.m. Why don't you go out and have a couple of cups of tea—no food, just tea." The woman thought, *This was just like my dream, where somebody was pouring warm tea on my hand and it was so refreshing.*

She realized that the Mahanta, the Inner Master, had been telling her in response to her singing HU, "Don't worry. Everything will be OK."

She sprang up from the chair just as if she were going to play a tennis match, and she ran out of the room. The tea settled her low-blood-sugar symptoms, and she was fine. At 4:00 p.m., the operation began.

The woman had been afraid of the general anesthetic. She didn't like it. It turned out that the doctor had changed his mind. "We're just going to use a local anesthetic," he said. She lay there quietly, feeling the scalpel cutting into her hand, wide awake, and sud-

Her sister had said, "When it's going past your twelve hours, remember to sing HU." So the ECKist began singing HU. She fell asleep and had a dream.

denly from nowhere, this brilliant white light shone right down on the operating table. The lights in the room got very much brighter. One of the nurses asked, "What's this?" The doctor and the nurse were seeing this white light too. The doctor began looking up at the ceiling, looking for the source of this very bright light that had come down and was supplementing the operating room lights.

The woman knew this bright light was the Light of God, a sign to her from the Mahanta. After the surgery was done, the surgeon said to her, "Your God is certainly close."

GOD IS WITH ALL OF US

A week later, the woman was scheduled for a follow-up examination with the same doctor in the outpatient clinic. When she came to the clinic, the doctor was delighted to see her. He looked at her hand, checked the wound, and saw that it was healing well.

Then he asked her, "What religion do you belong to?"

"Eckankar," she said.

"No wonder," he said. "I'm not surprised." In Africa, word of Eckankar has spread to so many different countries, from the very highest government levels all the way down to the very humblest people. The doctor explained what had happened in the operating room as he was ready to start surgery. He had been working so long that he must have had low blood sugar too, and his vision became impaired. And he was having trouble seeing her hand as he was trying to operate on it. Just as he was struggling, this bright light shone out of nowhere and gave him the extra light he needed to finish the operation.

The woman knew this bright light was the Light of God, a sign to her from the Mahanta.

The ECKist thanked the doctor. "God is with all of us," she said.

The light helped the doctor; but in helping the doctor, it helped the nurse and it helped the patient too. As she left the office that day, she gave the doctor an ECK brochure, and he was very happy.

Know that God's love is sufficient for you in all ways.

All of you are in the grasp of divine love. All the time, every day, no matter where you go.

So as you go home today, no matter what happens, know that you are in the grasp of divine love. Know that God's love is sufficient for you in all ways. And that if you need help, you don't even have to ask for it because this love is already with you.

The protection of God is as close to you as your heartbeat and as near to you as your own breath.

ECK Summer Festival, Sunday, June 16, 1996, Montreal, Quebec, Canada

No one on earth moves in a direct line toward a goal of any sort. We zigzag. We go up and down the hills, we go left and right, we take little detours.

10
FINDING WISDOM
FROM THE HEART

The theme for this morning is finding wisdom from the heart. Before we begin, I want to review what makes a good foundation for anyone who wants to go farther in the spiritual life. I'm referring again to the two laws of Richard Maybury.

Richard Maybury is a historian; he studies politics, economics, and law. He studied all the different commandments and laws that major religions have put together and boiled them down into two laws. His two laws don't cover everything, he recognizes that. But if people live by these two basic spiritual laws, they're going to have a good foundation for moving forward in their own spiritual life. The two laws of Maybury are: "Do all you have agreed to do" and "Do not encroach on other persons or their property." Once you learn that this is essential in the spiritual life, it creates a good foundation. Then you can go on; you can move into the higher areas, gaining spiritual wisdom and finding the wisdom from the heart.

The two laws of Maybury are: "Do all you have agreed to do" and "Do not encroach on other persons or their property."

HEART OF ANY TEACHING

No one on earth moves in a direct line toward a goal of any sort. We zigzag. We go up and down the hills, we go left and right, we take little detours. This is true whether we're trying to find our way back home to God or whether we're trying to learn how to live a fruitful life in this lifetime, to better ourselves, to be worth something. So that when our time comes to go, people will say, "He was a good man" or "She was a good woman."

What made us that? Essentially, it's as the New Testament says, "God is love." And as we say in Eckankar, Soul exists because God loves It. That means you exist because God loves you. This is the essence of truth. This is the heart of any teaching.

Soul exists because God loves It. That means you exist because God loves you.

DIFFERENCE BETWEEN US

The role of the Mahanta, the Living ECK Master is to show people in a way they can understand what these laws of Divine Spirit are. It's to understand and interpret the laws of Divine Spirit. There is really no difference between the ECK, Divine Spirit, and the Mahanta. But on the other hand, there is no difference between the ECK, the Mahanta, and each individual Soul. Because the Mahanta, as well as any other Soul, is created from the fabric of the Holy Spirit. The only difference for an individual Soul is the varying state of consciousness that one Soul has, compared to another Soul.

This is why we find such different behavior in this world. Even in the same church or the same congregation, among a group of people who supposedly believe the same thing, who take the same affirmations and follow the same creeds, you have people who range from very ethical, with a good way of treating their fellow human beings, to those who are on the opposite end of the ladder.

In every group you have people who are more advanced, more mature spiritually, and those who are less mature. That is life. There is no great leveler, such as socialism would have it, where you can make all people equal. It doesn't happen. People's states of consciousness are at different levels. People behave according to what they are, and they are all different. That's why we have this happy mix of people doing one thing or another.

LIVE BY THE LAW

Richard Maybury is a student of law and economics—two things that most people overlook. He studies law to see what was law in the past and what is law today. What is good law, and what is bad law. He studies economics to learn what is good economic principle and what is bad economic principle. He's found that when people in a society live according to the two laws, it is a good society.

If the law is right, if people understand how to live by the law—in other words, do all you have agreed to do, and do not encroach on other persons or their property—then there's going to be justice. And if people understand that economics means that you pay for everything you get, that there is no free lunch—if they can really understand, not just with their heads or mouth it with their lips, but live it—then it will be a sound society. If the law and economics of a nation, a country, or a people are sound, there will be justice. But when there is a prevailing mood of injustice, whether in the court system or in economics, where all sorts of wrong principles are

If the law and economics of a nation, a country, or a people are sound, there will be justice.

brought forth by the leaders, there is no justice.

What we're seeing today, especially, is such a lack of justice. Why? Basically, it's because the understanding of law and economics is bent and twisted today. Not the people's understanding, but that of many of the leaders of the people.

But with these two basic laws as guideposts, you can go on to the higher wisdom. You can start looking to find this wisdom from the heart.

You've got to have a good foundation. Otherwise you will not understand that some things make it and some things don't. If you know the principles of these two laws, you will at least have a guide for yourself.

Finding wisdom from the heart plays out in a number of different ways. Basically it's the relationship between you and Divine Spirit.

FINDING WISDOM FROM THE HEART

Finding wisdom from the heart plays out in a number of different ways. Basically it's the relationship between you and Divine Spirit.

The Mahanta is there to help you understand and interpret the voice of the Holy Spirit. Some people say, "Well, I can do that myself." But if people have just a very meager understanding of the laws of Spirit, have you ever heard them admit it?

We're all part of human nature. And human nature believes that whatever we know is the very best and highest. If people aren't growing, they will say, "This is it. My law is good enough for you." This is how they feel. If they don't have the highest understanding of life and you try to correct them, you stand to be corrected yourself. Don't try to correct people like this, because they'll come down hard on you. They become very angry, they become defensive, and they start throwing all forms of scripture at you until you wonder what hit you. Logically, they may be right. Logically, they may have a convincing argument that makes you silent. But unless you have love, you have nothing.

If you have love, you have everything. This is what we're trying to get at in these talks, in the teachings of ECK.

If you have love, you have everything.

HOW DIVINE SPIRIT SPEAKS

Divine Spirit will speak all the time through Light and Sound. Always through the Light and Sound. A couple from Minneapolis who work at the ECK Spiritual Center went for a trip to the West Coast. They wanted to go to Seattle, but they took a flight to Portland because it was cheaper. Then they rented a car to drive to Seattle.

They were on the freeway in the rental car, traveling in the fast lane. Traffic was going about eighty miles an hour. It was kind of a peaceful day. They had had a long plane flight, and they were kind of resting. The husband was driving; the wife was dozing in the passenger seat.

Suddenly for no reason the horn honked gently three times. The horn in the rental car just honked. It went, "Beep-beep-beep," as if it were speaking sweet little sounds to the couple.

The wife looked at her husband. "I wonder if the ECK is trying to tell us something," she said.

The couple drove on for a while, feeling a bit bewildered by what had just happened, when suddenly the horn honked again, "Beep-beep-beep." At this point, the couple went on full alert because they knew this was the Holy Spirit speaking to them. The Mahanta, the Living ECK Master helps people understand and interpret how Divine Spirit, or the Holy Spirit, speaks to all through the Light and Sound every second of every day.

They began to scan the freeway very carefully. Up ahead, a pickup truck in the fast lane had just lost power. It was slowing down very quickly. If they hadn't paid attention, the way it is with road hypnosis, they would have run into the back of the pickup.

The couple began to slow down so that the cars behind could also see that there was a problem. The driver of the truck was steering with his left hand and waving with his right hand through the back of the pickup, trying to get over to the shoulder of the freeway. He was able to do it, and an accident was averted.

The ECKists realized that the Mahanta had saved them from serious injury and possibly death. But it also occurred to them that the Mahanta had kept the truck driver from the same fate.

The reason they knew what to look for—when their car suddenly began to honk its horn—was that they knew about how these divine messages can come through and tell a person, "Pay attention." Because they had gotten this understanding from the ECK teachings, they knew what to look for in the way of Light and Sound.

LIGHT AND SOUND

Everything consists of Light and Sound in some form. Sound, or vibration interspersed with matter, creates matter of different density. It makes soft cushions, and it makes hard floors. It makes the plastic on this chair. It's a level of vibration, of the Sound going through matter of different composites to make another substance with has its own unique properties.

Everything consists of Light and Sound in some form.

And this is how the ECK speaks. It speaks in a number of different ways, including via dreams and intuition.

FINDING YOUR SPIRITUAL MISSION

On occasion I get a letter from someone who is not a member of Eckankar. Sometimes the people are getting the ECK teachings already, and it surprises them.

A woman wrote to me from Florida. She's not a member of Eckankar, but she has a friend who is in ECK. When they're talking, this person will sometimes tell the ECKist certain things. And the ECKist will say, "Why, that's straight from *The Shariyat*." *The Shariyat-Ki-Sugmad* is the bible of the ECKist. It means "Way of the Eternal." The ECKist was always surprised when her friend would come up with philosophies and statements of truth straight from *The Shariyat*.

Finally, this woman got interested in finding out what *The Shariyat* was. She had read a few of the other ECK books, but she hadn't really studied *The Shariyat*. So she began to read it. Not that long after, she had a dream.

In the dream, someone drove her to a distant meeting place. At this distant meeting place, there were a number of people gathered round. Among them was the Mahanta, the Living ECK Master. In the dream he came up to her and told her about part of her mission in this life. The woman had known she had a mission, but she hadn't been quite sure how it would play out.

When she woke up the next morning, this dream stayed in her mind. It struck her very strongly. To other people it would be just a dream, but to her it was not one of her usual dreams.

Shortly after this, she was in meditation. All of a sudden this little Chinese man came into her inner vision. He was dressed in blue. The woman didn't

In the dream he came up to her and told her about part of her mission in this life.

know it at the time, but it was the ECK Master Lai Tsi. First he was dressed in blue, but in an instant he was wearing a maroon robe and a happy little red cap. In her inner vision, he was dancing and laughing. She felt this enormous sense of joy and goodwill in her heart.

The woman wondered, *How can this little man have such power to bring so much happiness to me?*

Not long after that, she had an experience in the physical world, at Mount Shasta. This is often a gathering place of people who are interested in spiritual things. The people who gather there are both people in physical bodies and others who come in their Soul bodies or Astral bodies or sometimes Mental bodies. It's a gathering place for a lot of different people of different spiritual understanding. At this gathering, the woman met Gopal Das, another ECK Master. She noticed his twinkling blue eyes and his golden skin.

She said, "That's the man I met at Mount Shasta." Someone explained to her that he was Gopal Das.

About two years later, she and her friend went to an ECK center. There she saw a picture of Gopal Das on the wall. She said, "That's the man I met at Mount Shasta." Someone explained to her that he was Gopal Das.

She realizes that in this lifetime she has a mission to serve as an instrument for love, but as she goes along in the ECK teachings, she'll get a fuller understanding of what this mission of love is. She'll get a right understanding of it. And the right understanding is to become a Co-worker with God.

The only reason Soul exists is because God loves It. A Soul that recognizes this can do nothing other than to give love back to all life—to all the creatures and other beings here. She'll learn this. It's just a matter of spiritual unfoldment.

Learning by Doing

Many of you have been students of one or more of the ECK Masters in a past lifetime. That's why often I get letters from people who are not members of ECK who tell me they saw Lai Tsi or Gopal Das or Rebazar Tarzs or one of the other ECK Masters. Sometimes they don't know the name, or they get the name just a little wrong. But as soon as they see a picture of the ECK Master, they say, "That's the person who's been my guide all these years." This connection exists because that ECK Master was your beloved teacher at some time in the past when you were on the path of ECK.

Many of you have been students of one or more of the ECK Masters in a past lifetime.

People have come to the ECK teachings, and they have left the teachings too. They got as much as they needed at the moment, and then they had a falling out with the leader of the teachings of ECK at the time. The teachings may have had a different name outwardly, but they were the teachings of ECK. Students will become disgruntled or disillusioned, because they're looking at the world through the eyes of illusion. Often their teacher is trying to point out to them the way life really is.

There must be a balance between everyday living and the spiritual life. Otherwise a person is not living in harmony with Divine Spirit. I mention this because there are people who separate themselves from life.

Many years ago in Tibet, people would put themselves in little closed areas of contemplation or meditation. They would actually have a stone hut built around them, with a little place for food to come in every day if somebody fed them. Otherwise they'd starve inside their little beehive. This was how they spent their time. They thought by doing this they were more spiritual. But they were actually separating themselves from life. This is sometimes necessary for people to do, simply to get through the experience in that lifetime and find out it was not necessary to do.

But there is a lot of wisdom to be gained from doing. Most of you who are here, have been there. You've done all the far-out things that are possible to do in trying to reach God and find truth. You may have tried celibacy and other things. You may have practiced them not because it fit your nature, which is all right, but because of the ill-conceived notion that leading a celibate life makes you more holy in the sight of God than other people who are not celibate. And this is wrong. To do it for yourself is one thing. But if you do it so you can compare yourself to someone else and think you're better, it's a mistake. But, no problem. You've got a whole lifetime to work it out, or two or three if you want. Nobody's pushing you. There's no hurry.

EXPERIENCE WITH PAUL TWITCHELL

An ECKist from France had two dreams. These dreams were with Paulji. This is an affectionate name for Paul Twitchell, or Peddar Zaskq. Paul Twitchell was the founder of Eckankar in this present cycle, in 1965. Even though he translated, or died, in 1971, he's very active in the spiritual worlds. He is still helping me, as are many of the other ECK Masters, because they're helping you.

An ECKist from France had two dreams. These dreams were with Paulji.

This ECKist from France has a connection with Paulji. In the first dream, she was seated in a large room and a Satsang class was in session. Satsang is a study of spiritual scriptures. An ECK Master was conducting the class. All the other students in the class had a discourse in front of them, and they were studying it. The French woman, instead of having a discourse, had a pillow in front of her.

When she woke up, she was very upset. She wondered, *Why does everyone else have a discourse and I'm the only one in class with a pillow in front of me?*

Then she realized that she had been sleeping on the job. She hadn't been doing her spiritual exercises. She had not been reading her ECK discourses. Studying the ECK discourses is what gives you the spiritual food to take into your spiritual exercises. She realized she had been neglecting her spiritual disciplines, and she was able to do something about it.

Then the French ECKist had a second dream. This dream was totally in black and white. In the dream, she felt a sudden urgency to get to a bus stop because she knew that Paulji was going to be at this bus stop at a certain time. He was always there at a certain time. So she said, "I've got to get there." As she was crossing the street to get to the bus stop, she looked down and in her hand was a book: *The Spiritual Exercises of ECK.* The book's cover was full of color. The whole dream is black and white, but the cover of this book is in color.

As she was wondering about this, the woman looked up and saw a bus going by. In the bus was Paulji, and he waved to her from a window. She smiled and waved back.

The woman described him like this: a rather smallish man with twinkling blue eyes and a broad smile, because that is how Paul was many times. *What does this mean?* the woman wondered. *Why was the whole dream in black and white but* The

In the dream, she felt a sudden urgency to get to a bus stop because she knew that Paulji was going to be at this bus stop at a certain time.

Spiritual Exercises of ECK *was in full color?*
She got three lessons from the dream.

APPOINTMENT WITH DIVINE SPIRIT

The first lesson was that the spiritual exercises
were the colorful link between her and the ECK, the
Holy Spirit. The second lesson was that the spiritual
exercises gave her the means to meet the Mahanta
and the other ECK Masters, like Paulji. The third
lesson she got was that it's very important to do the
spiritual exercises at the same time each day. In this
instance, getting to the bus station at a certain time
each day. It's very important to do the spiritual
exercises at a certain time.

It's very important to do the spiritual exercises at a certain time.

If you are of the Christian faith, I might also say
that it's very important for you to say your prayers
at a certain time. Most of this is done by habit: prayers
before meals or, in some families, prayer after meals.
Prayers at bedtime. But always at a given time
because when there is an appointed time, it's like an
appointment between you and the source of truth,
between you and the Holy Spirit.

Say you have an appointment with someone, a
lunch date. You're looking forward to it. The lunch
date is at 12:00. You get there at 12:00, but the person
you're to meet doesn't get there until 1:00. What kind
of a lunch date is that? Something's very off. Or the
other person gets there at noon, and you get there
at 1:00. It's not going to be the happiest lunch hour.

It's the same sort of thing with your spiritual
exercises. When both parties are at a spiritual meeting
at the same time—like the Mahanta and you, or the
Christ Consciousness and you, or Divine Spirit and
you—it's like having an appetite for food. If you're
used to eating at noon, you're hungry by noon, and

you're going to appreciate the food more than if you ate lunch at 10:00, right after breakfast. Or if you ate lunch later. If you eat lunch one day at 10:00, the next day at 1:00, and the next day at 4:00, pretty soon your body is thrown completely out of balance.

If you want things to be in balance, if you want to be more in tune with the communication from the Holy Spirit, set a time. Make an appointment. This is the time to do your prayer; this is the time to do your meditations; this is the time to do your contemplations.

Being More Conscious

A housepainter lived on the East Coast of the U.S. He had never taken steps to build up his business because he thought he never would have that much business. He hadn't gone around looking for qualified painters to help him and let the business grow.

Yet he found it hard to say no to people. He kept saying yes to people who asked him to paint their houses. As time went on, he found that he had promised too many people. He couldn't do it all himself. And now he couldn't find the help to get all the work done.

He and his wife had three children at home, and there was a lot of food preparation each evening for dinner. He often helped with this. With all these pressures building on him, he wondered, *What am I going to do?* This often happens. We get ourselves into trouble in our daily lives because of some basic thing we haven't learned. In his case, he hadn't learned to say no. He got a lot of business, but he couldn't take care of it because he hadn't found painters to hire. It began to weigh on him.

As so often happens, when people have such

Make an appointment. This is the time to do your prayer; this is the time to do your meditations; this is the time to do your contemplations.

pressures from the outside world, it drives them to new spiritual understandings.

This man began to read *The Shariyat-Ki-Sugmad.* He found a passage in Book One on page 85: "Thus, the root source of error among lower beings is unconscious ignorance. . . . There is a remedy for this ignorance, for the Lord says, 'He who asks in my name shall receive all blessings, provided he is worthy. But if he is one who gives my message to the world and acts at all times in my name, he shall be among those who are indeed worthy and greatly blessed.' . . . Such blessings are often passed directly from the Mahanta, the Living ECK Master, to the chela." *Chela* means the follower of that spiritual leader.

He had a hard time understanding the words "and acts at all times in my name." *What does this mean?* he wondered.

He wasn't sure, but he kept doing the things that ECKists often do. You just say, "I do this in the name of the Mahanta." It can be something as simple as opening a door for someone else. For the painter, when he applied the first brush stroke to the house, he began to say, "I paint this house in the name of the Mahanta." Basically it meant he was going to do the very best he could.

You just say, "I do this in the name of the Mahanta."

He began going about his life, doing everything in the name of the Mahanta. That Saturday he went to an ECK workshop in a hotel. The topic was past lives. His wife was going to take their kids to music lessons, so she had the car. Before she left, she said to her husband, "Before the ECK workshop starts, would you please meet my friend and tell her that I wasn't able to come because the kids have music lessons?" Time was tight, but the man said, "OK, I'll do it." He jumped in the truck and took off for the hotel where the ECK workshop was to be held.

As he pulled up to the hotel and went inside the lobby, he saw a rather rough-looking man. This man was going from one person to another, offering them ten dollars to give him a ride to a high school in the area. And everyone he went up to said no. Maybe they were staying overnight in the hotel or maybe they were going to the workshop in just a few minutes. Or maybe they weren't sure it was safe to go with him.

The man came up to the painter. "Hey," he said, "would you give me a ride to the high school? I need to get there."

The ECKist said, "I'm supposed to meet a friend of my wife's here, and my meeting's going to start anytime."

But the man's case seemed compelling. The painter looked at him and thought, *This is a good person here, so I'll take my chances*. It flashed into his mind, *What would the Mahanta do in this case?* As he drove away from home earlier, he had been saying to himself, *Whatever I do today I'm going to do in the name of the Mahanta*. So he said, "Come on, let's go out to the truck. I'll take you."

It flashed into his mind, What would the Mahanta do in this case?

As they were driving to the high school, the passenger explained to the painter that an employment test was going to be administered at the high school. The man had to be on time or he would be disqualified. He had been able to catch a bus as far as the hotel. The bus didn't go any farther. He hoped he would be able to catch a ride from there. Someone had told him it was a two-mile walk to the high school, but he wasn't even sure where the high school was. As the man told these things to the painter, the painter was glad that he had given him a ride. This gruff-looking man was trying to make his own way; he was trying to get a job.

The passenger said, "Here, let me give you ten dollars." The painter said, "No, I don't want any money for it." "Well, at least let me give you five," the man said. The painter turned to his passenger and said, "This is my gift to you." He drove right to the front steps of the high school, let the man off, and said, "Good luck on your test."

The man looked at him. "You are a blessing of God," he said.

Just the way he had phrased it—not a simple thank you or God bless you—made the painter think back to these words from *The Shariyat:* "But if he is one who gives my message to the world and acts at all times in my name, he shall be among those who are indeed worthy and greatly blessed."

When his passenger had said, "You are a blessing of God," the meaning of this passage finally hit home. He now understood what it meant to do everything in the name of God. He was finding wisdom from the heart.

He now understood what it meant to do everything in the name of God. He was finding wisdom from the heart.

"I LOVE YOU, I LOVE YOU"

A Higher Initiate had been in Eckankar a long time. She had recently lost a younger sister to cancer. In the final days before the sister died, we say translated, her condition grew worse and worse. Finally the doctors decided to do an emergency operation. The sister was terrified of the operation. The ECKist wondered if she should have acted as more of a guardian for her sister against the intrusions of medicine. Her sister wasn't going to live anyway.

As the operation was about to begin, the sick woman said to the doctors, "Leave my body alone, and let me die." They kept interfering and interfering. All she wanted was peace. So she slipped into a coma, and the life-support systems were hooked up to her. After a few days, this younger sister finally died. The ECKist felt badly that she hadn't protected her sister more in the final days of her life on earth.

Several weeks later, the ECKist was sleeping in bed. In the middle of the night, she suddenly woke up in the Soul body. This feels more alive than waking up in the physical body or the dream state. If you are so lucky ever to awake in the Soul body, you find that you are more alive and more aware than you have ever been in your life.

Suddenly the woman heard a whirring sound. In experiences like this, there's usually some kind of a sound, which is one of the actions of the Holy Spirit. It's the power of the Holy Spirit working through Sound and Light. The woman went through an enormous black space. Little specks of light were moving past at a very great speed. She knew that the Mahanta was taking her to see her departed sister.

All movement stopped. Suddenly she was with her sister. They came toward each other. She could feel her sister's arms around her as surely as she had felt them in everyday life. "I love you, I love you," the sister said. And the ECKist said in return, "I love you, I love you."

When the first joyous meeting was over, the ECKist stood back and looked at her sister. She was thinking, *I wonder if she's going to some spiritual classes now that she's in heaven.*

She said to her sister, "By the way, are you taking any classes?" And her sister said, "Yes, cooking classes."

This caught the ECKist completely by surprise.

In the middle of the night, she suddenly woke up in the Soul body.

She realized that her sister was probably getting ready for her next lifetime when good food and nutrition would be even more important than it is today.

As our planet goes along, it's using up its resources. There will be a time we will find ourselves having to leave this planet. That is why there is this movement in scientific circles to go out into space and explore different planets. They have this instruction, this knowingness. They know we'd better go out there and start looking, because gradually this place is going to become truly a garbage can. It won't support life anymore. Its resources will have been all used up and wasted. Not real soon; don't expect it in your lifetime. These are long-range plans.

This woman was finding wisdom from the heart. She knew that her sister was all right. Whatever happened in the operating room in that last week of her sister's life really had no more bearing on anything. Her sister was happy. She was in heaven; she was doing what she liked to do. That's all that mattered.

She realized that surmounting all of this were the simple words, "I love you, I love you. I love you, I love you." This is all there is. If you can understand this with your heart and not with your mind, then you will have the essence of all truth that can ever be taught in any religion, including Eckankar.

We Keep Growing

An ECKist from England wrote me. He was telling me about how years ago when he was a young man, he was planning for his retirement. In those days, he said he still believed in retirement. You're young, and what do you do? You work your whole life so that someday you can retire. And do what? Wait? Just

She realized that her sister was probably getting ready for her next lifetime when good food and nutrition would be even more important than it is today.

stop living? As the young man grew up, he found a fallacy in the idea of retirement. Even though you retire from your job, you cannot retire from living.

A lot of people make that mistake when they retire from a job. In a way, they almost retire from living. This is when all their problems start to increase. Because they stop learning how to take care of themselves.

As we get older, our bodies don't respond the same way they used to. That means the foods and the nutrition that we were used to just aren't adequate anymore. Survival is a day-by-day lesson. It means you've got to keep learning, retired or not. Sometimes when people retire, they forget to keep growing in the areas of survival. They forget to ask, "How do I eat better?" or "What better nutrition do I need now? What isn't in the soil today that used to be there in 1940 when good food came straight from the land?" Things have changed. You've got to keep growing, because that's part of the spiritual law of survival.

LEARNING ABOUT LIFE

This man from England was learning all about finding wisdom from the heart through waking dreams. A waking dream is almost like one of Shakespeare's plays within a play. Something happens out here that gives you a snapshot of something that's going to happen in your daily life—either this week or in your future. It's a look at the future, a do-it-yourself, "try this at home" prophesy.

The Golden-tongued Wisdom is the action of the Holy Spirit coming through the Light or Sound and speaking through sometimes other people's words. For example, a person is talking about a party or going to the state fair. In the middle of their

The Golden-tongued Wisdom is the action of the Holy Spirit coming through the Light or Sound and speaking through sometimes other people's words.

conversation, something lights up in gold lights about a spiritual principle that you had been thinking or wondering about. That's the Golden-tongued Wisdom.

This man from England also gets this wisdom from the heart through radio, TV, and the press. The Golden-tongued Wisdom will come out sometimes, as he listens to TV or reads something, giving him some insight into his spiritual life. It's Divine Spirit's way of communicating with him. It's another form of prophecy, personal do-it-yourself-at-home prophecy.

Dreams? These are another way of finding wisdom from the heart. Once you begin looking sincerely for truth—and it doesn't just mean people who are on the ECK path—you begin having dreams that lead you to some avenue of truth. They give you insights. Dreams are seeing through a glass darkly, for the most part.

Soul Travel is living life at its fullest without having to look through any glass, clear or not. You are there. This physical world often is looking through a glass with smudges on it. As Soul, in Soul body, you don't look through a glass of any sort. You're there in full consciousness, which is what we try to lead you to at some point.

Dreams? These are another way of finding wisdom from the heart.

A BETTER RETURN

The man from England bought a piece of land in India for his retirement. The rest of his family was still living there on it. But when his father died in 1994, the surviving members of the family forgot who had originally bought this land. He had bought the land. It should all be his. But the father had used it for so long that the surviving family members just said, "It's the father's. We're going to divide this land up equally now." So the man got just a little sliver of his original investment.

The man was thinking, *Bum luck*. He was all the way over in England. He knew it was going to be tough getting his land back.

But, then one day he got an insight. He was finding wisdom from the heart. He realized that HU, this word that you sing as a love song to God, is the source of all life. The ECK, which is the Word of God, has gone out from the Sugmad, which is the highest God. This Word has created all lands, all physical matter in every physical world. At the same time this man knows of the Shabda. This is yet another word found in the world religions for the Word of God, or the Holy Spirit.

He realized that HU, the name of God, was his to sing anytime. It's his way to make a direct link with the Word of God, singing the name of God. He looked this over and decided that the gift of HU was a much better return on his investment than a piece of land in far-off India. He was finding wisdom from the heart.

First, get a good foundation in your spiritual life, so that you have a platform from which to go into the higher worlds. Maybury's laws are: "Do all you have agreed to do, and do not encroach on other persons or their property." These refer to outer laws. But the greatest law of all is the Law of Love. And this is the law that you're interested in to find your way back home to God.

May the blessings be.

First, get a good foundation in your spiritual life, so that you have a platform from which to go into the higher worlds.

ECK Worship Service, Temple of ECK, Chanhassen, Minnesota, Sunday, September 1, 1996

GLOSSARY

Words set in SMALL CAPS are defined elsewhere in this glossary.

ARAHATA. *ah-rah-HAH-tah* An experienced and qualified teacher of ECKANKAR classes.

CHELA. *CHEE-lah* A spiritual student.

ECK. *EHK* The Life Force, the Holy Spirit, or Audible Life Current which sustains all life.

ECKANKAR. *EHK-ahn-kahr* Religion of the Light and Sound of God. Also known as the Ancient Science of SOUL TRAVEL. A truly spiritual religion for the individual in modern times. The teachings provide a framework for anyone to explore their own spiritual experiences. Established by Paul Twitchell, the modern-day founder, in 1965. The word means "Co-worker with God."

ECK MASTERS. Spiritual Masters who can assist and protect people in their spiritual studies and travels. The ECK Masters are from a long line of God-Realized SOULS who know the responsibility that goes with spiritual freedom.

GOD-REALIZATION. The state of God Consciousness. Complete and conscious awareness of God.

HU. *HYOO* The most ancient, secret name for God. The singing of the word HU is considered a love song to God. It can be sung aloud or silently to oneself.

INITIATION. Earned by a member of ECKANKAR through spiritual unfoldment and service to God. The initiation is a private ceremony in which the individual is linked to the Sound and Light of God.

LIVING ECK MASTER. The title of the spiritual leader of ECKANKAR. His duty is to lead SOULS back to God. The Living ECK Master can assist spiritual students physically as the Outer Master, in the dream state as the Dream Master, and in the spiritual

worlds as the Inner Master. Sri Harold Klemp became the
MAHANTA, the Living ECK Master in 1981.

MAHANTA. *mah-HAHN-tah*   A title to describe the highest state of
God Consciousness on earth, often embodied in the LIVING ECK
MASTER. He is the Living Word. An expression of the Spirit of
God that is always with you.

PLANES.   The levels of existence, such as the Physical, Astral, Causal,
Mental, Etheric, and Soul Planes.

SATSANG. *SAHT-sahng*   A class in which students of ECK study a
monthly lesson from ECKANKAR.

SELF-REALIZATION.   SOUL recognition. The entering of Soul into the
Soul Plane and there beholding Itself as pure Spirit. A state of
seeing, knowing, and being.

THE SHARIYAT-KI-SUGMAD. *SHAH-ree-aht-kee-SOOG-mahd*   The
sacred scriptures of ECKANKAR. The scriptures are comprised of
twelve volumes in the spiritual worlds. The first two were
transcribed from the inner PLANES by Paul Twitchell, modern-
day founder of ECKANKAR.

SOUL.   The True Self. The inner, most sacred part of each person.
Soul exists before birth and lives on after the death of the
physical body. As a spark of God, Soul can see, know, and
perceive all things. It is the creative center of Its own world.

SOUL TRAVEL.   The expansion of consciousness. The ability of SOUL
to transcend the physical body and travel into the spiritual
worlds of God. Soul Travel is taught only by the LIVING ECK
MASTER. It helps people unfold spiritually and can provide proof
of the existence of God and life after death.

SOUND AND LIGHT OF ECK.   The Holy Spirit. The two aspects through
which God appears in the lower worlds. People can experience
them by looking and listening within themselves and through
SOUL TRAVEL.

SPIRITUAL EXERCISES OF ECK.   The daily practice of certain techniques to get us in touch with the Light and Sound of God.

SRI. *SREE*   A title of spiritual respect, similar to reverend or pas-
tor, used for those who have attained the kingdom of God.

SUGMAD. *SOOG-mahd*   A sacred name for God. Sugmad is neither
masculine nor feminine; It is the source of all life.

WAH Z. *WAH zee*   The spiritual name of Sri Harold Klemp. It means
the Secret Doctrine. It is his name in the spiritual worlds.

INDEX

239

FOR FURTHER READING AND STUDY

The Art of Spiritual Dreaming
Harold Klemp

Dreams are a treasure. A gift from God. Harold Klemp shows how to find a dream's spiritual gold and how to experience God's love. Get insights from the past and future, grow in confidence, and make decisions about career and finances. Do this from the unique perspective of being able to recognize the spiritual nature of your dreams.

A Modern Prophet Answers Your Key Questions about Life
Harold Klemp

A pioneer of today's focus on "everyday spirituality" shows you how to experience and understand God's love in your life—anytime, anyplace. His answers to hundreds of questions help guide you to your own source of wisdom, peace, and deep inner joy.

The Spiritual Exercises of ECK
Harold Klemp

This book is a staircase with 131 steps. It's a special staircase, because you don't have to climb all the steps to get to the top. Each step is a spiritual exercise, a way to help you explore your inner worlds. And what awaits you at the top? The doorway to spiritual freedom, self-mastery, wisdom, and love.

35 Golden Keys to Who You Are & Why You're Here
Linda C. Anderson

Discover thirty-five golden keys to mastering your spiritual destiny through the ancient teachings of Eckankar, Religion of the Light and Sound of God. The dramatic, true stories in this book equal anything found in the spiritual literature of today. Learn ways to immediately bring more love, peace, and purpose to your life.

Available at your local bookstore. If unavailable, call (612) 544-0066. Or write: ECKANKAR, Dept. BK18a, P.O. Box 27300, Minneapolis, MN 55427 U.S.A.

THERE MAY BE AN ECKANKAR STUDY GROUP NEAR YOU

Eckankar offers a variety of local and international activities for the spiritual seeker. With hundreds of study groups worldwide, Eckankar is near you! Many areas have Eckankar centers where you can browse through the books in a quiet, unpressured environment, talk with others who share an interest in this ancient teaching, and attend beginning discussion classes on how to gain the attributes of Soul: wisdom, power, love, and freedom.

Around the world, Eckankar study groups offer special one-day or weekend seminars on the basic teachings of Eckankar. For membership information, visit the Eckankar Web site (www.eckankar.org/membership.html). For the location of the Eckankar center or study group nearest you, click on "Other Eckankar Web Sites" www.eckankar.org/ekcenters.html) for a listing of those areas with Web sites. You're also welcome to check your phone book under **ECKANKAR**; call **(612) 544-0066, Ext. BK18B;** or write **ECKANKAR, Att: Information, Dept. BK18B, P.O. Box 27300, Minneapolis, MN 55427 U.S.A.**

☐ Please send me information on the nearest Eckankar center or study group in my area.

☐ Please send me more information about membership in Eckankar, which includes a twelve-month spiritual study.

Please type or print clearly

Name _____
    first (given)   last (family)

Street_____ Apt. # _____

City _____ State/Prov. _____

ZIP/Postal Code _____ Country _____

About the Author

Sri Harold Klemp was born in Wisconsin and grew up on a small farm. He attended a two-room country schoolhouse before going to high school at a religious boarding school in Milwaukee, Wisconsin.

After preministerial college in Milwaukee and Fort Wayne, Indiana, he enlisted in the U.S. Air Force. There he trained as a language specialist at Indiana University and a radio intercept operator at Goodfellow AFB, Texas. Then followed a two-year stint in Japan where he first encountered Eckankar.

In October 1981, he became the spiritual leader of Eckankar, Religion of the Light and Sound of God. His full title is Sri Harold Klemp, the Mahanta, the Living ECK Master. As the Living ECK Master, Harold Klemp is responsible for the continued evolution of the Eckankar teachings.

His mission is to help people find their way back to God in this life. Harold Klemp travels to ECK seminars in North America, Europe, and the South Pacific. He has also visited Africa and many countries throughout the world, meeting with spiritual seekers and giving inspirational talks. There are many videocassettes and audiocassettes of his public talks available.

In his talks and writings, Harold Klemp's sense of humor and practical approach to spirituality have helped many people around the world find truth in their lives and greater inner freedom, wisdom, and love.

International Who's Who of Intellectuals
Ninth Edition